CASS

ABOUT THE AUTHOR

Jon S. Baird was born in Aberdeenshire in November 1972. He was raised in Peterhead, a local fishing port, and worked for his late father's roofing firm before graduating from the University of Aberdeen. In the 1990s, he moved to London to pursue his ambitions as a filmmaker. Baird started his television career as a runner for the BBC, quickly progressing to work as a freelance director for every major UK network. His short film, It's a Casual Life, about the football 'casual' scene, led to employment on the feature film Green Street. It was here that he met Cass Pennant, whose life story he was immediately drawn to. Their subsequent collaboration, CASS, written and directed by Baird, has been hailed as a remarkable first feature and a future British cult classic.

Illustrated Screenplay
by Jon S. Baird

CASS

THE MOVIE

**The ultimate behind-the-scenes guide
to a remarkable British cult film**

Pennant Books

First published in paperback 2008
by Pennant Books

Screenplay © Jon S. Baird/Cass Films Ltd 2008
'An Interview with Jon S. Baird' copyright © Jon S. Baird/Cass Pennant.

Based on the book *CASS*
By Cass Pennant & Mike Ridley

British Library Cataloguing-in-Publication Data:
A CIP record for this book is available from
The British Library

ISBN 978-1-906015-31-2

Design & Typeset by Envy Design Ltd

Printed and bound by 🐾 Grafica Veneta S.p.A., Trebaseleghe (PD) - Italy

Commissioning editor: Cass Pennant
Project editor: Paul Woods

Pennant Books
A division of Pennant Publishing Ltd
PO Box 5675
London W1A 3FB

www.pennantbooks.com

For everyone who helped
make this possible

CASS: THE PUBLIC'S RESPONSE

For anyone growing up in the 70's and 80's, football headlines revolved around violence and gang war, rather than Beckham's new hairstyle. It burned into anyone's memory . . . as did the memory of English teams being banned from international competition . . . The ICF (the Inter City Firm's name based on the modes of transport – rail and vans – used to get to away games to meet their foes) had a fearsome and growing reputation; one group of the ICF was headed by Cass Pennant, who stumbled upon violence as his way of gaining respect during a difficult childhood in a ridiculously racist country. This is the story of a general turned gentle by family values and just plain old growing-up and is one of the best films of its time, easily equalling *Quadrophenia*'s view of England . . . A remarkable and brilliantly-played fact-based drama that completely epitomises its subject matter . . . Superb!
Paula Westwood – www.sofacinema.co.uk

. . . It gives an insight into the football violence but it is much more than that – this is the man's life. The underlying positive messages of 'family' and 'responsibility' . . . [are] more powerful and more meaningful than anything a politician's got to say . . . The two main women in his life seem to have a massive influence and are portrayed with enormous respect and affection. I think we all had similar relationships with our fathers in the 70's/80's to the one portrayed in the film! Proper film; proper geezer.
Ken P – Birmingham

Finally a film that tackles the issue of racism without being politically correct. I'm fed up with seeing films and TV programmes that show only white characters as racists with no criticism of the attitudes that can sometimes be found in the black community. This film turns that around and does it in a way that avoids patronising any section of society.
Hoolifan – www.imdb.com

Watched it in Manchester . . . packed and buzzing. The film's a great story and very real, I went through every emotion watching it, I laughed, I cried, I shuddered, I cheered, I punched the air, and I came out thoroughly satisfied.
Carl S – Oldham

Saw film in Brum, great film, blinding casting, good storyline, and true realism. Thought-provoking, deeper than you first think. It just goes to show . . . if you ain't happy with your lot then change it! (No one ever died from falling in water; they only die if they ****in' STAY in it!)
John P – Wolverhampton 6

. . . It was great to see Frank and lots of 'hard b*****ds' and a who's who of good British actors in it, and not to mention the big man himself . . . My screening was absolutely rammed, and it was great to see people of all walks of life there! Fantastic job, really entertaining and can't wait to see the sequel!!
Dee – West London

I've been waiting to catch the movie and get all the books since I hear about Cass, on *The Robert Elms Show*, what a turnaround! Very, very proud of you, brother. May the almighty grant you long life so we can enjoy your positivity more and more . . . say amen to that!
Ray – Charlton (Nigeria)

(For further, unaccredited reviews, see **www.casspennant.com**)

CASS: The Contents

INTRODUCTION:
CASS: THE MAKING OF . . .
An Interview with Jon S. Baird   1

CASS: THE MOVIE   20

CASS: THE AFTERMATH . . .
An Interview with Jon S. Baird   252

Credits: 261
Cast   261
Crew   262
Music   266
With thanks to: 269
With special thanks to: 270

INTRODUCTION

CASS: THE MAKING OF . . .
An Interview with Jon S. Baird

It was March 2004. I was working on *Green Street* as an associate producer when the director came up with the idea of getting Cass Pennant involved as a technical consultant.

I'd heard all about Cass and the exploits of the Inter City Firm, so I was really wary of him at first. I didn't really know that much about his story apart from the violent side. I certainly didn't realise he was a reformed character.

Cass gave me a copy of his book. I took one look at the cover and thought, "Oh no, here we go, another East End hard man story." I wasn't going to say that to his face obviously, so I thanked him and smiled politely.

On the train home I read the first two chapters and was taken completely by surprise, because there was nothing there about football violence. It concentrated on how he had been shot and, as a result, how he'd suffered posttraumatic stress disorder, but the most interesting part to me was when the story jumped back to his childhood. It explained how he was adopted by white parents, and how he'd been given the girl's name Carol by his biological parents. I thought, "This isn't at all what I'd expected. There is something really different here. This is a story of a man's identity struggle."

How did you get the job on Green Street?
I'd always wanted to work in the film industry but it's very difficult to break into, especially if you're not based in the South of England. When I was twenty-four I moved down to London from Aberdeen and got a job at the BBC as a runner, which is pretty much a glorified tea boy. I worked my way up in the BBC comedy

department, but I always wanted to do drama and ultimately film, so I had to make a break. The then Head of Comedy had said to me, "Look, go and do a short film and showcase your talent." So I went off and did a short film called *It's a Casual Life*. It's about a guy looking back on his days as a football casual, and how much the scene has changed since the 1980's.

Was that personal to you?
It was personal because I'd grown up in Aberdeen and there was a big casual scene up there.

When I was doing *Casual Life*, our scriptwriter, Dougie Brimson, was also working on *Green Street*. He asked the director, Lexi Alexander, to come down to the set to see how we filmed the big fight sequences. Lexi must have been quite impressed because she then asked me to work on *Green Street*.

Through Lexi I met Stefan Haller, who eventually became the producer of *CASS*. Stefan is very confident, very articulate and very charming, so I first thought, "He's really different from me. There's no way I will be

able to work with this guy." Three years on he's become a really close friend.

Stefan had never produced a feature film before, but like me who'd never written or directed one, he talked a good game! He was trying to convince me that he was a good producer and I was trying to convince him that I was a good director, but we were both slightly naïve to say the least, at the time. Stefan had worked for Warner Brothers in script development, so he knew the studio system and I think his confidence spurred me on. "How are we going to get the money, Stef?" "Oh, we'll get the Film Council, we'll get somebody. Don't worry!"

So why would the Film Council be interested in your film?

I think we really ticked all the Film Council's boxes. It was a British story; it was a true story; it was a period piece; it was about social history; it was about race; it was about adoption, and it was a story of redemption. All those themes ran through it and all sang from the Film Council's hymn sheet. However, we also had the

'H' word, and the 'H' word is worse than the 'C' word in Britain. You mention anything to do with hooliganism and it just turns most people off. "Sorry, don't want to know." I can understand their reasons, so I didn't take it personally. The person who really got this film made, as far as financiers within the film industry were concerned, was Will Clarke from our distributor, Optimum Releasing. Our major financier came from outside the industry, but Will was the only person who believed in us from day one, really.

Is it normal to get a distributor before you've made your first film?
As first-time filmmakers, to get a distribution deal before you've even shot a roll of film is very unusual. Both Optimum and another major distributor wanted the film, so it gave us a lot of confidence. Optimum also understood that it wasn't just another hooligan movie, which was very important to us.

So why do you think they picked up on it?
I sent them the *CASS* script and we arranged to meet them out in LA, at the American Film Market. They said at the meeting, "Yeah, we'll have it." We really couldn't believe how smoothly it all went. Optimum stayed with us through the highs and lows, and believe me, there were some lows.

Like what, for example?
Our major financier pulled out of the film on my wedding anniversary – which was a difficult day, I can tell you. I was preparing to go away for a weekend with my wife, and I got this email saying that they'd withdrawn all of their £1.2m investment. That was a real blow. They also wrote an extremely harsh criticism of the script, and it felt like a personal attack on me at the time.

I think naivety really helped us get through it, because we just thought, "We're going to make this film, we're going to raise the money, of course we will." It was probably just through blind confidence that *CASS* got made, and the persistence of a few individuals: Cass Pennant, Stefan and me being the core of that.

There also had to be a lot of trust between us, because Stefan and I put hundreds of thousands of pounds into a bank account without signing any deal and without having any contract. Either one of us could have walked off with the whole lot. It was all done on a gentleman's handshake.

What was the first defining moment in the whole process?

The first real defining moment came in February 2005. I was on holiday in the Caribbean, and I remember picking up the *CASS* book, reading it over and over from start to finish repeatedly. It was at that point I thought, "I want to make this story my first feature film."

Did you stick tightly to the script when shooting the film?
You've got to have discipline on your set, but not so much that it confines creativity. You try to get a balance. When you're shooting a film across five decades, if you've only got twenty-five days to complete it and you don't have a proper plan you're going to get yourself in trouble. You've got to have a tight script and schedule and stick to it as much as you can.

Were you always going to write the script?
I'd never written a script before so we spoke to quite a few writers, but we weren't happy with the situation for one reason or another. I think eventually Stefan said to me, "Well, why don't you write it?"

I'd already spent a year with Cass Pennant, getting to know him, so Stef said, "There's nobody who knows the story better than you, you know these characters, you know who Cass is." That's how it happened. Anyway, I don't think we would have found another scriptwriter who would have had the time to get to know Cass, and who could have gained the trust that we really needed from him.

Stefan was always going to be a good script editor for me because that's what he'd done previously, whilst working at Warner Brothers. He usually gave really thorough script notes, but on the odd occasion they were sometimes as basic as, "This is shit – please do better!"

The script was emailed back and forth from LA to London: "Please do better," "Please do more," "Fuck you, Stef!" "Fuck you, Jon!" He flew over here, I flew over there. Who the hell did we think we were? We had a laugh doing it though.

Yours and Stefan's director-producer partnership is unusual.

Stefan developed the script with me and I worked with him to produce the film and raise the finance. Usually a producer wouldn't have worked so closely on a script and a writer/director wouldn't have worked so closely on the producing side, but there was nobody else – just the two of us.

It was a very difficult time in my life at that point, because I was engaged to be married and my dad was

really unwell. Then my dad died the week before my wedding, so I lost a lot of my confidence around that point. I think writing the *CASS* script was really therapeutic. It helped get me through a really difficult stage because I could lose myself in my own little world for ten months.

My wife knew exactly what I was going through. If I didn't have her, this film wouldn't have been made, that's the bottom line. If she hadn't been so under-standing I'd probably be divorced by now. She must have thought I was having an affair with Cass, the amount of time I spent with him! My sister and mother were also very important. They, along with my wife, gave me the moral and financial support that I needed to make the film.

What were you looking for in the script? There are so many strands to the story.
It was always going to be a story of identity. I wanted to drop a lot of the football stuff, which we did. The first draft of the script was a hundred and fifty pages, and we still hadn't finished it. That was because we tried to put everything in there. I didn't realise the work that was involved in writing a script, before I started on *CASS*. To write a page takes forever – one page, never mind a full draft. The prison sequence had taken me nearly a month to write and it was sixty pages long. We chopped forty pages out of it with one click of a delete button. That's soul destroying, but it was a case of, "Well, what do we do? We just cannot afford to shoot all of that." Those sacrifices need to be made when you go through the script development process.

How long did the script take to write?
We were writing right up to the last day before the shoot in September 2007, and I started in October 2005. There was a great film director called Alexander

MacKendrick, who was behind a lot of the Ealing comedies, and a great phrase that he used was, "A good script is never written. A good script is written and rewritten, and rewritten, and rewritten, and rewritten."

How much of the structure had changed from the original?

There were a few big characters we had to lose, but the general story was there. We changed locations, rewriting little bits of scenes right up until the day before we started shooting. It's all about keeping only the most necessary stuff in there and having as little 'fat' as possible. Everything else seems more interesting once you get rid of the padding.

The next major part of the process was finding the right cast. We had a few people in mind straightaway. Leo Gregory [FREEMAN] I knew from *Green Street*. He was first on the team sheet. Stefan really wanted Tamer Hassan [RAY] to be involved and when I met him I saw why, as he's a really charismatic guy. Stefan had seen Tamer in a film called *The Business** and he was really impressed by his screen presence. He said, "This guy IS a movie star."

Did you have a role for them, or did you just want to get them?

No, no, it had to be a role. We'd never say, "Oh if we can get him, we'll find a role for him." I don't believe in that. It was always Leo for FREEMAN and Tamer for RAY. Those were the first two names on the cast list. The character of CASS was always going to be a big problem. There are a lot of good black actors in Britain, but finding somebody with the physicality was going to be extremely difficult.

* *The Business* (2005) – Nick Love's Brit gangster flick set on the 'Costa Del Crime', with Danny Dyer.

Did he have to be British?

To me, accents are one of the first things that I always pick up on. If you don't get the accent right, then you can't believe the character. That happened in *Green Street* and it wasn't going to happen in my film. It was always going to be an all-British cast. It's very, very difficult for another nationality to do a decent British accent. One of the only times it's worked was with Rene Zelwegger in *Bridget Jones*. The voice coach we employed for all three of our actors who played CASS at varying stages of his life was Barbara Berkeley, who had done *Bridget Jones*.

I knew of Nonso Anozie from his theatre work and I also knew he was doing *Atonement*. I'd heard he was also going to work with Mike Leigh, so I thought, "This guy must have something special about him." Then my sister phoned me up and said, "Have you seen *The Times*' Top Fifty actors to look out for?" Nonso was in there – a six foot six black man, one of the only black actors named. When we met him we thought, "This is the guy." So it was a culmination really of his theatre work, his CV, and the expectations that people had for him.

How important was it that your CASS had to look like the real character?

The physicality was extremely important because the real Cass is so tall and well-built. We knew what Nonso had done on stage, but we just wanted to make sure he could do it on film. Nonso is actually bigger than the real Cass, and there aren't many actors who are.

Black actors in this country are never really given lead roles. You name the last one that had a lead role in a British film. It doesn't usually happen, especially in a biopic. We sent his agent the script and he came to meet me and Stef in a hotel in London. We were sitting waiting in the lobby bar, and Nonso walked through

the door wearing this long coat. I said to Stefan, "Here's CASS, coming through the door. This is unbelievable, look at him!" He'd got the physicality; he just needed to do the rest. Nonso completely exceeded our expectations in the film, he is an exceptional actor.

So you were happy with your cast?

Gavin Brocker [PRENTICE] was an unknown quantity at that point, but after the first week the crew were calling it *The Gavin Brocker Show* because he was so good.

Nathalie Press [ELAINE] was an idea from our casting agents, Julie Harkin and Suzanne Smith. We offered the part of ELAINE to Nathalie. We didn't audition anyone for that part. We saw her in *My Summer of Love* and thought that she'd be great.

Paul Kaye [CP] was an idea of mine, as was Ralph Ineson [SERGEANT MULLINS]. Bronson Webb [THE ASSASSIN] was again introduced through the casting agents. Bronson's worked with some massive directors – Ridley Scott and Christopher Nolan, to name but two.

Lorraine Stanley [LINDA] I'd seen in *London to Brighton* and I thought she was brilliant. Jamie Kenna [STEVIE HOGAN] I'd worked with on *It's a Casual Life* and *Green Street*.

I don't know what Verelle Roberts [YOUNG CASS] had done before, but he just came in and blew us away in his audition. Nonso gets all the credit and rightly so, because he's fantastic, but a lot of that is because Verelle puts in a tremendous performance at the start of the film to build the foundations of the CASS character.

Doll and Cecil were important characters as well though?
Linda Bassett [DOLL] and Peter Wight [CECIL] were two actors that I was aware of, but I didn't realise how talented they actually were. I think they provide two of the strongest performances in the film. They were amazing at subtly portraying DOLL and CECIL's relationship. Linda and Peter weren't available for rehearsals, but with the relationship they had on screen you would have thought we had weeks with them. They just turned up on set and did their thing, and were both consummate professionals. When Cass Pennant's foster sister, Beverley, saw the finished film, she was crying at the end and said how much Peter and Linda were like her foster parents – the real Doll and Cecil Chambers. That really meant a lot to me.

What's it like when you're about to start shooting your first feature film?
That was another defining moment – leaving my house in Surrey with two bags of possessions over my shoulders. Chris Ross, the director of photography, said to me, "When you do your first film, it's like going to war." It sounds silly now, but that's exactly what it felt like at the time, walking to the train station and on my way to London to get ready for five weeks of war!

For the limited budget at our disposal we had to shoot the film in twenty-five days – which really was three or four days under what we should have had. We also planned to shoot on weekends because that's when all the extras were going to be available. The extras that we

used were real people, they weren't from an agency. They were friends and family of mine and of Cass. They really made the film real for me. They gave it the authentic look that we could not have achieved with professional extras.

What were the first few days of shooting like?

The first day was 26th September 2007. I got a phone call before I arrived on set saying, "Why have the actors not got any trailers?" People were kicking off. I just thought, "Oh for fuck's sake, what is going on here?" This was at six o'clock in the morning. Thankfully, we didn't have a lot of problems like that after the first day.

I met Cass just outside the dining bus and we stood there looking at each other. We started laughing, going, "What have we got ourselves into?" It was good because Cass gave me a little pep talk, saying, "Come on, we've got this far, we've got to do it." We never really looked back after that.

The first two days were really important for us, because we knew we had to get off to a strong start and not fall behind the tight schedule. We started with the interior scene of the van going up to Newcastle, and also the fight scene in the café where CASS gets stabbed – quite big scenes really. We got through the first two days without any major hitches – apart from Paul Kaye breaking his ribs and Gavin Brocker breaking his fingers. All in a day's work really!

CASS

DIR: JON BAIRD

CAM: CHR

SCENE

73 PT

SLATE

36

TA

DATE:

27 SEPTEMBER 2007

A

CASS
The Movie
BY JON S. BAIRD

EXT. THE ALBANY NIGHTCLUB CAR PARK – NIGHT
1993
There are two big black doormen, BIGS and FRANK,
standing at the entrance to the club. The ASSASSIN
and CP's GANG wait in a parked car.

INT. ASSASSIN'S CAR – NIGHT
The GANG snort cocaine and appear aggressive. THE
ASSASSIN sits in the front passenger seat. In the driver
seat is the GANG leader, CP.

> CP
> My old man says he's a nigger and
> he's West Ham, so do him twice.

THE ASSASSIN removes a silver handgun from the glove
compartment.

THE ASSASSIN
I'm gonna blow the black bastard's
fucking head off!

CP puts a calming hand on THE ASSASSIN'S shoulder.

CP
(clinically)
Aim for the chest, not the face.

EXT. THE ALBANY NIGHTCLUB CAR PARK — NIGHT
The Taxi draws up in front of the club and the door
opens. CASS gets out and approaches the Club where
BIGS and FRANK are waiting. The ASSASSIN, CP and
gang approach.

ASSASSIN
You black West Ham cunt.

BANG! CASS is shot.

FADE TO BLACK.

OPENING TITLES

> CASS V/O
> The last place I wanted to die was
> south of the river in Millwall
> country, Low Life City. I was a man
> who'd experienced more violence
> than you'd ever want to in a
> thousand lifetimes, so I always
> thought I'd go out fighting. I'd
> been shot, stabbed and kicked
> senseless, but I'd handed out my
> share of retribution 'n' all. It'd all
> been part of the game up till then.
> The film you're about to see is
> based on a true story, my story.

OPENING TITLES END

EXT. WOLVERHAMPTON SUBWAY – DAY 1972*
YOUNG CASS walks through a subway with YOUNG
FREEMAN and YOUNG PRENTICE. They're now 14

---

*We started off the film with a real funky soundtrack from Booker T and the MGs called
'Melting Pot', which we also used over the end credits. It was a really good way to
introduce the seventies, because as soon as you hear that music you realise the period
you're in, you see the clothes and go back to that particular time. JSB

years old and are wearing WEST HAM UNITED colours.
YOUNG CASS is the leader.

> YOUNG CASS
> ... so Kevin's with his bird up in
> her bedroom and her old dear's
> just fucked off down the pub, so he
> thinks, "I'm quids in here, mate." So
> he starts to try and get her bra off.

The BOYS start to chuckle.

> YOUNG PRENTICE
> (excited)
> What? So he can feel her tits?

YOUNG CASS stops and gives YOUNG PRENTICE a look.

> YOUNG FREEMAN
> No, so he can put her bra on his
> head! Of course so he can feel her
> tits you soppy bastard!

YOUNG FREEMAN laughs as YOUNG PRENTICE looks
embarrassed.

> YOUNG PRENTICE
> I was only asking.

YOUNG FREEMAN shakes his head and laughs.

> YOUNG FREEMAN
> I worry about you mate.

They continue walking and YOUNG CASS resumes his
story.

YOUNG CASS
So, he's having a fucking
nightmare and he gets his jumper
caught in her bra-fastener things.

The BOYS giggle in anticipation.

YOUNG CASS (CONT'D)
Well his bird's had enough of this
and starts to push him off, but
he's stuck to her now and can't get
free. Anyway, the two of them are
wrestling around on the fucking
ground.

YOUNG PRENTICE
What a prick.

YOUNG FREEMAN
You can just imagine them, like
Big Daddy and Giant Haystacks.

YOUNG CASS
Anyway, her fucking dog comes
into the room and thinks he's
attacking her. So it bites him in
the bollocks!

YOUNG FREEMAN
What a wanker!

YOUNG PRENTICE
Stupid little cunt.

YOUNG CASS
What a bell end, mate.

As they exit, a gang of 20 Wolverhampton Wanderers supporters, the WOLVES, violently beat up FOUR WEST HAM SUPPORTERS. One of the WOLVES urinates on a WEST HAM supporter. The BOYS panic, hide their scarves under their jumpers and run back into the subway.*

The BOYS exit the other end of the subway and stop running as 10 WEST HAM MOB appear, the same guys from the pub scene. The WEST HAM MOB run towards the BOYS, thinking they're WOLVES.

> WEST HAM MOB LEADER
> (excited)
> Come on, do the Wolves nigger!

---

* The night before we shot this scene, the production designer, Daniel Taylor, had been painting the subway with 1970s graffiti. 1970s graffiti and 2008 graffiti are obviously not alike, to say the least. He'd been painting, "Coons go home," or something equally as racially offensive. Daniel is quite a thin, blond, angelic-looking lad who also wears glasses – he looks like the Milky Bar Kid. He turned round and there were these three black kids on bikes with their hoods up, staring at him completely disbelievingly, shaking their heads. "What the fuck are you doing?" Dan said, "It's for a film." They replied, "We don't give a shit if it's for a film! You can't do that!" So he had to paint over the whole thing again and then wait until the morning, when he and the art director went to retouch it. I'm surprised that he never got killed! Seriously though, we wanted to keep it as authentic as possible and it was Cass who told us, "The racist slurs at the time were very heavy, and for the effect to be real, it has to be as gruesome as possible."

The costume design will help define your period more than anything else. I didn't really know the seventies fashions as well as I did the eighties, so I took a lot of my advice from Cass. Guy Speranza, the costume designer, went through a lot of books and spoke to Cass about it. Everybody who remembers that period tells me it looks authentic – the donkey jackets, leather jackets, Dr. Martens, scarves tied round the wrist, long hair, graffiti on the walls. Most of the colours as well, because firms wore colours in the seventies which they stopped doing in the eighties. It was really important for me to achieve the right look.

That scene was filmed on the last day of our first week. I think the extras thought they'd only have to fight once, but I think it was about take 18 or 19 as the light faded! Those guys had put themselves through hell to make our film look authentic. I can only sincerely thank them for doing that. JSB

The BOYS are scared and stand frozen in fear. YOUNG CASS quickly holds up his West Ham scarf like a shield.

> YOUNG
> CASS/PRENTICE/FREEMAN
> (shout nervously)
> We're West Ham!

The WEST HAM MOB come to a stop just before they attack. They look at each other and start to laugh.

> WEST HAM MOB LEADER
> Who you then? Clyde Best's little
> brother?

The MOB crack up laughing at the joke. The BOYS are silent.

> WEST HAM MOB LEADER (CONT'D)
> You ain't West Ham if you're on
> your toes from them muggy dingle
> Wolves.

YOUNG FREEMAN
They're a proper mental firm,
mate. They just kicked the fuck out
of some West Ham geezers.

WEST HAM MOB LEADER
Fuckin' northern monkey cunts!

YOUNG PRENTICE
They were pissing on this one
geezer!

The MOB LEADER grabs YOUNG PRENTICE.

> WEST HAM MOB LEADER
> Shut up, you mug, just show us
> where they are or I'll piss on you,
> you little cunt.

YOUNG CASS stands up for his friend.

> YOUNG CASS
> Leave it out mate. They're only on
> the other side.

The MOB LEADER starts to walk at a very unusual fast pace. He bounces as he leads THE MOB into the subway, smashing into the WOLVES who have appeared.

YOUNG CASS, YOUNG FREEMAN and YOUNG PRENTICE are just bystanders. The MOB LEADER fights with the WOLVES LEADER. TWO WOLVES jump on the MOB LEADER'S back and bring him to the ground.

YOUNG CASS instinctively springs into action, smashing his two feet into the ribs of one of the WOLVES. YOUNG PRENTICE and YOUNG FREEMAN join the fight briefly, but stop and run as they hear a police siren. YOUNG CASS seems not to hear the siren and fights viciously.

YOUNG CASS is consumed with violence, continuously kicking a WOLVES fan. A POLICEMAN restrains him.*

---

* It was typical low-budget filmmaking, flying by the seat of our pants. Daniel Kaluuya's [YOUNG CASS] wig kept falling off during the fight, and the makeup department had to keep gluing it back on. His trousers were also falling round his arse, and his flares and big Cuban heels were tripping him up, but he never complained once. He was brilliant. When the POLICE arrived, running in like the Keystone Kops, they were well up for a ruck – at first. When they ran down the tunnel and were out of shot, some of the extras turned on them and started really beating them up. They were soon shouting, "No, stop, we're only actors!" JSB

EXT DOLL CHAMBERS' HOUSE
1958
DOLL, a white woman in her late forties, pushes a pram
and turns into her front path. A PASSER-BY walks past
and stops. The PASSER-BY peers inside the pram and
we see a 6-month-old black baby, BABY CASS.

> PASSER-BY
> Oh isn't he a sweetheart?

DOLL smiles at the PASSER-BY and picks BABY CASS up.

> DOLL
> Yes love, he's a real darling.

> PASSER-BY
> They're still cute at that age,
> aren't they? Before they get that
> curly hair and them big lips.*

DOLL is furious and holds BABY CASS tight. The
PASSER-BY is unaware of the offensive comment as she
walks off.

> PASSER-BY (CONT'D)
> Bye then love.

DOLL marches up the stairs.

INT DOLL CHAMBERS' BATHROOM – DAY
DOLL lifts BABY CASS into the sink and gently washes
his skin.

---

* In the scene where the PASSER-BY comments on the "curly hair and them big lips" of
BABY CASS, Linda Bassett's reaction is so strong that you know from the very first
minute that DOLL's a tough old dear. That particular line was never intended to be
funny, but for some reason it got a massive laugh at the screenings – especially from a
black audience. It's set in 1958 and a lot of younger people now might not realise that's
what it was really like. That kind of attitude was common back in those days. JSB

FADE OUT.

INT. DOLL CHAMBERS' BATHROOM – DAY
1968
We see a close-up of YOUNG CASS's arms. He is now 10 years old and is washing his hands and lower arms in the sink. He scrubs his skin furiously as if trying to remove a stain.

> DOLL (O.S.)
> (shouts)
> Come on, love. You're going to be late again!

YOUNG CASS presses his face against the mirror and stares deeply at his own reflection. He stares at his skin and thumps the wall in frustration.*

INT. DOLL CHAMBERS' DINING ROOM – DAY
CECIL CHAMBERS, a white man in his late fifties, sits at the kitchen table with his wife DOLL. YOUNG CASS enters. He is wearing short shorts but it is not summer. He picks up some toast and heads for the door.

> DOLL
> Oi! Ain't you going to sit down and have something?

YOUNG CASS turns round with a sombre look.

> YOUNG CASS
> I'm going to be late, mum. Like you said.

---

*When YOUNG CASS is trying to scrub the black colour off his skin, it alludes to what has happened to him in between those years – the torrent of abuse that he's had to suffer. The beginning of the film is top heavy with racism and aspects of race because it was a very important part of Cass's life. We show YOUNG CASS being in a state of depression as a kid, but trying to hide it from DOLL and CECIL. It's a very sincere, serious beginning to a so-called 'hooligan film'. JSB

DOLL
Oh come on, son, I've made your
favourite especially.

YOUNG CASS shrugs.

YOUNG CASS
Sorry mum, I ain't hungry.

DOLL
You're never hungry, what's wrong
with yer? Cecil, tell him to eat
something.

DOLL pushes CECIL'S arm, making him spill his tea.

CECIL
(flustered)
Come on son, don't upset your mother.

YOUNG CASS
(anxious)
I got to get going.

DOLL
You just behave yourself, right?

DOLL fastens his shirt collar.

DOLL (CONT'D)
And don't be out with your neck
all open like that. You'll catch your
death out there!

YOUNG CASS leaves.

EXT. RAILWAY OVERPASS – DAY
YOUNG CASS walks along a railway overpass. A group
of OLDER TEENAGERS and a boy YOUNG CASS's age,
BILLY, laugh and wait at the other end for him. The
OLDER TEENAGERS swing bicycle chains and carry
bits of wood. They encourage BILLY.

BILLY
Golliwog.

TEENAGER 1
How the fuck do you comb that
fuzzy wuzzy hair?

TEENAGER 1 spits in YOUNG CASS's face and TEENAGER
2 punches him in the balls. YOUNG CASS completely
ignores them.

TEENAGER 2
Where do you come from then,
chocolate face?

BILLY runs behind YOUNG CASS and kicks him up the
arse.

BILLY
Fucking blacky.

BILLY looks to the OLDER TEENAGERS for reassurance.

TEENAGER 1
(laughing)
You tell him Billy.

YOUNG CASS wipes the phlegm off his hair and face.
He is tormented but suppresses it.

BILLY
Oi, nig-nog. We found a photo of
you. Want to see yourself?

BILLY takes out a black jack wrapper from his pocket and shows the TEENAGERS, who laugh hysterically at the golliwog image. YOUNG CASS stares back at them.

> TEENAGER 1
> He's got a granny as a mum 'n' all.

> BILLY
> Yeah, what happened to your real mum, monkey boy?

> TEENAGER 2
> Don't you remember? We fed her last week at London Zoo.

> TEENAGERS
> (monkey chants)
> Ooo ooo ooo ooo!

BILLY squares up to YOUNG CASS.

> BILLY
> My dad says you lot should go back to where you come from. Go on, fuck off back to the jungle!

Two of YOUNG CASS's friends, YOUNG PRENTICE and YOUNG FREEMAN, appear.

> YOUNG FREEMAN
> Fuck off Billy, you gypo.

BILLY sneers at YOUNG FREEMAN.

> BILLY
> (mocks)
> What you pair of cunts doing

hanging about with a darkie for
anyway then?

BILLY turns back to face YOUNG CASS.

> BILLY (CONT'D)
> Ain't you going to say nothing . . .
> Carol?

YOUNG FREEMAN and YOUNG PRENTICE are nervous,
but encourage YOUNG CASS.

> YOUNG FREEMAN
> Go on, Cass.

YOUNG PRENTICE
Do him, Cass.

YOUNG CASS lunges for BILLY. They start to fight.*

CASS V/O
From day one, Prentice and
Freeman were always there for me.

INT. DOLL CHAMBERS' BATHROOM – DAY
DOLL stands by the sink cleaning YOUNG CASS's injuries.
His clothes are torn.

DOLL
That's another new school uniform
ruined. I can't afford to buy a new
one every week, you know! You
can't just go around fighting with
people all the time.

YOUNG CASS
(frustrated)
It's not my fault, mum.

DOLL looks at him, then continues to tend the wounds.

DOLL
What happens if someone reports
you to Dr Barnardo's?

---

* Cass Pennant took me back to Slade Green and showed me the location where he was bullied and tormented, not only for his skin colour, but also for his name. The child actors found it difficult to get to grips with the script, because the racial slurs were foreign to them. Cass had a chat with them and told them how important it was that they made it look as serious as possible. The kids who played the aggressors performed their parts brilliantly. When you see YOUNG CASS coming over the railway overpass, wearing his short shorts, it immediately gives you the feeling of what he's going through at home. He must have thought, "I've got a girl's name, I'm the only black kid for miles around, my mum's fifty and she's making me wear these fucking shorts. Everyone else has names like Paul, or Bob, or Dave, and they're wearing long trousers. Now how much more different could I be?" JSB

YOUNG CASS shrugs.

> DOLL (CONT'D)
> I tell you what happens. They'll
> say I can't control you. They'll
> bloody well take you away from
> me, that's what happens. Is that
> what you want, Carol?

> YOUNG CASS
> (shouts)
> Stop fucking calling me that name!

DOLL slaps YOUNG CASS.

> DOLL
> Don't you ever talk to your mother
> like that. You hear me?

> YOUNG CASS
> (crying)
> Well don't you ever call me Carol
> again. It's not my name and I'm
> not going to answer you if you call
> me that anymore. I'm sick of being
> tormented for it. It's a girl's name,
> everyone knows it's a girls name.

> DOLL
> It wasn't me that gave you that
> name so don't blame me, blame
> them that gave you away!

> YOUNG CASS
> You don't have to call me that name.
> I can't take it anymore. Why can't
> you call me something else then?

DOLL
Well what am I supposed to call
you, you daft sod? I can't just call
you 'son' all the time.

YOUNG CASS
Call me Cass.

DOLL
Call you what?

YOUNG CASS
Cass. Call me Cass.

DOLL
Cass? What's that?

YOUNG CASS
That's what my mates call me.

DOLL
(laughs)
Why on earth do they call you
that? That's worse than Carol.

YOUNG CASS
(upset)
No it ain't. It's after the boxer.

DOLL
What boxer?

YOUNG CASS
The American one. Cassius Clay.

DOLL
Bleeding hell, I might have known

it would have something to do
with fighting.

YOUNG CASS
Yeah, but he's the best, he's the
toughest fighter there is. I want to
be famous like Cassius Clay.
Everyone likes him.

DOLL
People don't like you just 'cos you
can bash people up, son.

DOLL picks up YOUNG CASS's school report and reads
from it.

DOLL (CONT'D)
You ain't thick, love, see: "Car . . . is
disruptive in class and seems
easily distracted, however he has
shown great promise in creative
writing which he should spend
more of his time on." See, even the
teachers know you ain't a dummy.

YOUNG CASS
Yeah, but all the kids apart from
my two mates think that all I am
is a darkie.

DOLL grabs him and hugs him tight.

DOLL
You're my special boy.

YOUNG CASS
(unsure)

Special, like Cassius Clay?

DOLL winks at him.

> DOLL
> Just like Cassius Clay.

CASS responds with a smile.*

INT. DOLL CHAMBERS' LIVING ROOM – DAY
DOLL zips up YOUNG CASS's coat and wraps a West Ham
United scarf round him. CECIL waits patiently.

> DOLL
> Right, you pair, off you go.

DOLL looks at YOUNG CASS but points at CECIL.

> DOLL CONT'D
> And don't you let him take you
> down that pub with his West Ham
> mates! No bad influences, right?

CECIL goes to leave, YOUNG CASS follows.

> DOLL
> (concerned)
> Look after him, Cecil. I don't want
> him getting into any more trouble.
> You hear me?

---

* My favourite scene in the film is the bathroom scene with YOUNG CASS and DOLL. We saw about two hundred kids for the part and none of them came close to Verelle Roberts. His performance in this scene is so accomplished for a young actor.

I thought the way Chris Ross shot that was cinematically beautiful. Our music composer, Matteo Scumaci, put some beautiful music to it and called it 'Doll's Theme'. We play it again when CASS comes out of jail, and also at DOLL's funeral. It gives a great reflection of the bond between mother and son. The photography is beautiful. The acting is brilliant. The music is fantastic. We were very proud of that scene. JSB

CECIL
He'll be alright, Doll, it's only the football.

They leave.

INT. ANNE OF CLEVES PUB – DAY
CECIL and YOUNG CASS sit in a busy pub, full of WEST
HAM SUPPORTERS.

CECIL
So you excited about the game, son?

YOUNG CASS
(suspicious)
What's the special occasion then?

CECIL
Eh?

YOUNG CASS
Why you taking me with you all of
a sudden?

CECIL
Your mother thought we should
spend a bit of time together.

YOUNG CASS
Why?

CECIL
(awkwardly)
You know what your mother's like,
son.

CECIL tries to change the subject. He is uncomfortable.

CECIL (CONT'D)
Anyway, who's your favourite West
Ham player?

YOUNG CASS
Not sure.

CECIL
Come on. Bobby Moore, Martin
Peters, Geoff Hurst?

YOUNG CASS
Don't know.

CECIL
Oh well, don't matter. Just
remember to keep close to me
today. I don't want you getting
hurt. Right, Cass?

CECIL winks and nudges YOUNG CASS, who responds
with a smile. CECIL lifts his drink to his lips.

CECIL (CONT'D)
(under his breath)
Your mother'd kill me.

The West Ham Fan song master, BUBBLES, starts singing.
The pub falls silent.

BUBBLES
I'm forever blowing bubbles, pretty
bubbles in the air. They fly so high,
they reach the sky and like my
dreams they fade and die.
Fortune's always hiding, I've looked
everywhere. I'm forever blowing
bubbles, pretty bubbles in the air.

EVERYONE
United, United, United.

YOUNG CASS gasps in awe. He's instantly hooked. A MOB of men approach CECIL and YOUNG CASS. One is the WEST HAM MOB LEADER.

CECIL
(hesitantly)
Alright, fellahs?

WEST HAM MOB LEADER
(slightly dismissive)
Yes mate.

The MOB stare at YOUNG CASS and smirk at each other. The WEST HAM MOB LEADER bends down and stares at CECIL and YOUNG CASS, then sighs and shakes his head.

WEST HAM MOB LEADER (CONT'D)
(sarcastic)
I don't know what the fucking East
End's coming to. Do you?

CECIL is nervous. YOUNG CASS looks to him for support.

CECIL
(apologetically)
Come on fellahs, he's only a little
kid.

The MOB walk off laughing. CECIL smiles at YOUNG CASS.

CECIL (CONT'D)
(unconvincing)
You alright son?

YOUNG CASS turns away. It's clear he doesn't have the same respect for CECIL that he has for DOLL.*

EXT. THE ANN OF CLEVES PUB – DAY
It's the following Saturday. YOUNG FREEMAN, YOUNG CASS and YOUNG PRENTICE approach the pub entrance. They're hesitant.

YOUNG PRENTICE
We going in or what then?

YOUNG FREEMAN
Ah fuck it, we're half on the firm now!

The BOYS laugh and go to enter the pub. A drunken PUB REGULAR stops them before they enter.

PUB REGULAR
Oi. There's no fucking nig-nogs allowed in this pub. Stick with the sambos' snooker club up the road.

The BOYS look stunned. Suddenly the PUB REGULAR is punched to the floor. The WEST HAM MOB LEADER towers over him.

---

* Probably the most convincing location for portraying the time period is the Britannia pub, especially in the sixties, when CECIL takes YOUNG CASS to the football for the first time. You go in there and it's smoky, they're wearing the flat caps, they're drinking out of pint dimple mugs, they're smoking No. 6, they're wearing scarves. It's just so East End.

It's a dramatic scene which shows how alienated the kid is, how foreign YOUNG CASS was in that environment. When CECIL says to YOUNG CASS, "You stick close to me today because I don't want you getting hurt," it's followed by a lot of silences which took me back to my childhood a bit, because my dad took me to the football and he was older than the average parent as well. I remember him saying stuff like that to me, so I think that piece of dialogue must have come from somewhere deep in my own childhood memories. JSB

WEST HAM MOB LEADER
Fuck off you nonce. He ain't a nig-
nog. He's one of us. He's West Ham.*

The WEST HAM MOB LEADER turns to the BOYS.

WEST HAM MOB LEADER (CONT'D)
Well don't just fucking stand there.
In you go.

The BOYS are elated and walk into the bar.

INT. THE ANN OF CLEVES PUB – DAY 1983

There has been an obvious time shift when CASS,
FREEMAN and PRENTICE enter. They are now in their
early twenties and wear 'casual' style clothes. They are
greeted with respect by their male counterparts, the ICF,
as they slowly make their way through the crowd. They go
to the bar. In the corner of the pub sits RAY, who is slightly
older and is wearing a suit.

_____

* One of the funniest moments in the film is the head-butt outside the pub, because
it's quite unexpected. Dave Lea, our fight arranger, constructed a great stunt there.
I thinking the take that we used for the head-butt, Jamie Kenna, who plays STEVIE
HOGAN, actually butted the guy. It wasn't a full-on head-butt, but he definitely
connected and that's why it looks so real. JSB

RAY
Oi oi, it's Duran Du-fucking-ran!

CASS motions to FREEMAN and PRENTICE and the boys all approach RAY. The BOYS greet RAY and sit down slowly beside him. It's obvious they have respect for him.

CASS
Thought you'd been nicked, Ray?

RAY
(winks)
I got bail, didn't I?

CASS
How much they fix your bail at then, mate?

RAY
Twenty.

PRENTICE
Twenty grand?

RAY turns to PRENTICE.

RAY
No, twenty quid. Of course twenty
fucking grand. And they took my
fucking passport 'n' all. They'd set
me up, the cunts. There's no way
I'm getting off with this one.

CASS
What d'you reckon you'll get?

RAY
They'll give me ten easy for this
one, but I'll probably do five.

CASS
Five years? Fuck that.

RAY shrugs. It's no big deal.

RAY
Anyway, thought I'd make the
most of it while I can. Know what I
mean?

RAY winks, then sinks his drink and motions to the
bar for another.

RAY (CONT'D)
You ain't still wasting your money
following the Hammers, are yer Cass?

CASS
Too fucking right, mate. Splice me
open and you'll see my claret is
claret and blue.

RAY
I just stick to the boxing now,
mate. I couldn't bear to go and
watch them getting fucking served
up any more, Cass.

FREEMAN
You won't have to worry about that
for a while though, eh Ray?

FREEMAN laughs to emphasise it was a joke, but RAY
turns to him slowly. He is not laughing.

RAY
(deadpan)
What d'you mean by that, son?

FREEMAN starts to get nervous.

FREEMAN
Nothing, Ray. I was only kidding, mate.

RAY
You taking the fucking piss, are yer?

FREEMAN is now really worried.

FREEMAN
Ah fuck, look, I'm really sorry, Ray.
I never meant to offend yer, mate.

FREEMAN looks at the floor. RAY leans over the table towards him.

> RAY
> (quietly aggressive)
> Just as fucking well then.

CASS and PRENTICE look worried, but RAY winks at them. They realise he's been winding FREEMAN up. There is silence, as FREEMAN has still not looked up. CASS, RAY and PRENTICE are trying to hold in their laughter, but crack up as FREEMAN looks up. It takes a moment before he realises and sighs with relief. RAY ruffles FREEMAN'S hair.

> RAY (CONT'D)
> Fucking 'ell. You alright, son?

FREEMAN lets out a sigh of relief.

> FREEMAN
> Fuck me. You proper had me there, Ray.

EVERYONE is now laughing.*

---

* *This scene is when we're first introduced to RAY. We always wanted RAY to be a subtle character. We needed something to show that he was a serious player, so it was perfect for a Joe Pesci–Ray Liotta moment between RAY and FREEMAN. I won't disguise the fact that it was a device influenced by GoodFellas. It's more admiration than plagiarism of Martin Scorsese!*

The Britannia is actually the pub that the Inter City Firm used back in the day, so you couldn't get any more authentic than that. The landlord of the Britannia – he's a very interesting looking guy – was chuffed, because it's tucked away in a part of east London where probably not that much happens most of the time. The only thing we had to change in the Britannia was to take the Sky dish off the wall. You could have been in the fifties, sixties, seventies or eighties in that pub, because it hadn't changed at all since then. Some of the film critics commented on how realistic the locations are. I wanted to film in the East End and I wanted to film at the real locations, so the Britannia ticked all the right boxes. JSB

CASS V/O
Unlike Ray, we were only one-day-
a-week gangsters.

INT. WAREHOUSE – DAY
CASS and FREEMAN are working as painters.

CASS (V.O.)
When Monday morning arrived, we
were no different from any of the
rest of Maggie's Miserables. An
honest day's work for a dishonest
day's pay. During the week we were
just another cog in Thatcher's
square wheel. You had to give
yourself something to look forward
to at the weekend.*

The works GAFFER approaches them aggressively and
addresses CASS.

---

* The scene with the painters and decorators was the hardest for me to shoot. It'd been
a really long day and, for some reason, it just wasn't working. It was one of those scenes
where you just thought it was awful at the time, but it turned out alright once we'd
placed the sound design to get a bit of context.

One of the most difficult things as a director is when you know that everybody else
knows it isn't working, and it's up to you to pull it round. Everybody's looking to you. It
must have been the same for Cass or someone like Bill Gardner during the ICF days, when
it was all on top. Guys would look to Bill and Cass for guidance. That's what it feels like as
a director. You've got to hold it together, you've got to be the one steering the ship. JSB

GAFFER
Get a fucking move on for fuck's
sake, you're two days behind. You
can forget about making your
fucking bonus for a start. What is
it with you people, eh? Your sort
are all the fucking same. No good
and fucking lazy.

INT. OFFICE – DAY
PRENTICE sits behind a desk twiddling a pencil. He looks
extremely bored and continuously stares at the clock.

CASS (V.O.)
Even office workers like Prentice
couldn't wait till the bell rang on a
Friday afternoon, so they could get
their weekly fix of the ultraviolence.*

ARCHIVE FOOTAGE OF HOOLIGAN FIGHT.

CASS (V.O.)
And it wasn't only us cockneys
either. Every Saturday, up and
down the country, armies of young
men battling each other in the
streets, in the pubs and on the
terraces, to defend their home
territory. All in name of their
sacred football clubs.

---

* We wanted to include this scene because we needed to show how these guys, the
Inter City Firm, weren't all tradesmen or labourers or unemployed, but they had
clerical jobs too. That's why we wanted PRENTICE to be an office worker looking bored
at work, to give the idea that there was nothing else going on in their lives.
   I chose Gavin Brocker because you can believe him as an officer worker, but also
because you can see his energy, which is important in the fight scenes. PRENTICE is
the most ferocious out of the three boys. We always wanted to do that, to show that the
office guy was the most dangerous. JSB

ARCHIVE FOOTAGE – INTERCITY 125 TRAIN
A train travels through a grim northern landscape.

> CASS (V.O.)
> We'd ditched the piss-drenched
> soccer special trains every other
> mob was travelling on and went
> North to South on the newer,
> faster, more stylish Intercity 125's.
> It was what we were all about.

EXT. LEEDS HOUSING ESTATE – DAY
We start on a close up of CASS and slowly pan out to
reveal PRENTICE, FREEMAN and THIRTY ICF.

> CASS (V.O.)
> Designer clothes and designer
> violence, just another product
> of 1980's Britain. The papers
> called us 'le thugs nouveau', and
> our Inter City Firm – being full
> of lads from the East End and
> Essex – were more 'nouveau'
> than anyone else. We were the
> famous, the famous ICF, and
> humiliation was the business
> we specialised in.

They see a LEEDS SPOTTER who also sees them. He starts to run and a small group of ICF break away and chase him. CASS leads the main group in the other direction.

INT. LEEDS PUB – DAY
The pub is packed with LEEDS FANS.*

> LEEDS FANS
> (singing)
> Marching on together!

The LEEDS SPOTTER enters and approaches the LEEDS LEADER, whispering in his ear. The LEEDS LEADER nods.

> LEEDS LEADER
> How many?

The LEEDS SPOTTER whispers in his ear again. The LEADER stands up.

> LEEDS LEADER (CONT'D)
> (shouts)

---

* *The Leeds Service Crew were one of the most notorious firms back in the day. A lot of the previous football-related films never really concentrated on the northern clubs. We wanted to include Leeds, Wolves and Newcastle, because nobody had used these before. We got Cass Pennant to contact Stoke, and they agreed to come down and play the Leeds.*

The Leeds fight should have been huge in the film, it should have been massive. There were two reasons for it not being so: one was that we completely overstretched ourselves, and thought we could shoot a lot more in a day than we actually could. The second was because of a communication error. The Leeds/Stoke guys hadn't been told that they were to just come over a fence and stop. They charged over the fence and didn't stop until they came face to face with their West Ham foe. All hell broke loose as they smashed into each other. Our leading actors, Nonso, Gavin and Leo, were right there in the mix. One of the Stoke boys came in with a snide punch to Leo and it all kicked off! I really thought we'd have to shut down for the day and get Leo off to hospital, because we thought he'd broken his cheekbone. The guys from Stoke were really embarrassed, because they didn't know who it was in their group who'd done it. There was an air of tension because some of the West Ham lads wanted revenge. They were getting out their mobile phones, wanting to call down all the heavies from the East End. If that had happened there would have been World War III! JSB

Fucking cockneys are here! Fifty of
'em!

The pub empties as all the LEEDS FANS charge out the
door to confront the ICF.

LEEDS FANS
(chanting)
Leeds, Leeds, Leeds!

EXT. LEEDS HOUSING ESTATE – DAY
CASS, FREEMAN, PRENTICE and the main group walk
back through the estate. On the other side of the estate
LEEDS appear. There is a standoff. The ICF fan out,
arms folded.

ICF
(chanting)
ICF ... ICF ... ICF ...

LEEDS
(chanting)
Leeds, Leeds, Leeds!

They smash into each other.

INT. LEEDS PUB – DAY
The pub is quiet and empty as the LEEDS LANDLORD
sweeps up the mess. The LEEDS fans enter and their
expressions change from joy to horror as the pub has

been torn to pieces. There is smashed glass everywhere, and table and chairs lie strewn across the floor.

> LEEDS LEADER
> (furious)
> Fucking dirty cockney bastards!

The LEEDS LEADER rushes out the pub with the LEEDS gang.

FADE OUT

EXT. CASS & FREEMAN'S FLAT – MORNING
PRENTICE approaches, carrying the Sunday newspapers. He knocks on the door.

INT. CASS & FREEMAN'S FLAT – MORNING
The letterbox opens and we see PRENTICE'S eyes peering in.

> PRENTICE (O.S.)
> Wake up you lazy cunts.

INT. CASS & FREEMAN'S FLAT, LIVING ROOM – MORNING
It's quiet but there is evidence of a party. FREEMAN and
CASS emerge from separate rooms in their underpants.
They are hungover and bruised from the fight.

> FREEMAN
> You get your end away then?

> CASS
> Nah, says she had a boyfriend and
> fucked off about twelve. You?

FREEMAN thrusts his hips forward.

> FREEMAN
> Fucking right mate, I was at it all
> fucking night. She knows what her
> fanny's for, that's for sure. What's
> that now, four nil for me? You'll
> have to start watching your Uncle
> Freeman to get some tips, Cass.

> CASS
> (laughs)
> Fuck off.

PRENTICE knocks on the door.

> PRENTICE (O.S.)
> Come on, you pair of slags, put your
> cocks away for half a minute and
> open the fucking door, will yer's?

FREEMAN leaves the room and we hear him open the
door. He enters with PRENTICE, who carries the newspapers. PRENTICE surveys the messy room.

                    CASS
                    OK mate, you've had an eyeful,
                    what's all the fucking fuss for?

                    PRENTICE
                    (disappointed)
                    Two page two's and a page four.

                    CASS
                    (angry)
                    Who gave us a page four?

                    PRENTICE
                    The Observer.

                    FREEMAN
                    Posh cunts.

PRENTICE sits.

                    PRENTICE
                    (annoyed)
                    Chelsea got the front pages again.

CASS looks furious.

                    CASS
                    (shouts)
                    Fucking Chelsea!?

FREEMAN and CASS grab the newspapers, reading the
headlines.

                    CASS (CONT'D)
                    (angry)
                    'Notorious Chelsea hooligans'?
                    What a lot of fucking bollocks!

FREEMAN
Listen to this, 'Mindless thuggery
as West Ham mob attack Leeds
pub'!

CASS
Mindless? We'd planned that for
weeks.

The boys laugh. TRACEY enters. She is topless but
wearing jeans.

TRACEY
Where's my fucking top, Freeman?

PRENTICE and CASS cheer and
wolf-whistle.

PRENTICE
Reenie! Reenie!

TRACEY
(annoyed)
My name ain't Reenie, right! It's
Tracey.

CASS
(laughs and chants)
Reenie! Reenie!

TRACEY
Where's my bra then?

FREEMAN picks her bra up off the floor and holds it up.

TRACEY (CONT'D)
Give us it then!

FREEMAN
(laughs)
Come and get it.

TRACEY walks over to get it, but FREEMAN throws it to
PRENTICE. TRACEY is getting pissed off.

TRACEY
Stop fucking about.

PRENTICE goes to hand it to TRACEY but, as she tries to
grab it, he throws it to CASS, who catches it and laughs.

TRACEY (CONT'D)
(sneers)
Get your filthy hands off it.

PRENTICE realises it's a racist remark.

>   PRENTICE
>   You fucking little slag.

>   TRACEY
>   (snaps)
>   What are you, his fucking
>   boyfriend are yer?

FREEMAN intervenes. He walks over to TRACEY calmly.

>   FREEMAN
>   Hold on, hold on. It's all my fault.

FREEMAN suddenly grabs TRACEY and pushes her out
of the room.

INT. CASS & FREEMAN'S FLAT, HALLWAY – DAY
FREEMAN shoves TRACEY out the flat and closes the door.

>   TRACEY (O.S.)
>   Let me in you little prick!

FREEMAN opens the door. TRACEY pleads desperately.

>   TRACEY (CONT'D)
>   (unconvincing)
>   I'm sorry, alright?

FREEMAN smiles, then throws her bra and top at her.

>   FREEMAN
>   Me too, darling. Now fuck off and tell
>   that pikey cunt of a Millwall boyfriend
>   of yours that the ICF'S done his little
>   Reenie up the 'arris again!

FREEMAN slams the door.

INT. CASS & FREEMAN'S FLAT, LIVING ROOM – MORNING
FREEMAN enters, there is silence. CASS looks upset.

> FREEMAN
> Don't worry about that little slut,
> mate.

> CASS
> (angry)
> I don't give a shit about her. I'm
> pissed off about that fucking
> kiddie firm stealing all the
> headlines again.

CASS stands up and marches round the room. He rips
up a newspaper and throws it on the floor.*

> CASS (CONT'D)
> (forcefully)

---

* This scene was shot during the couple of days we had on an estate on south London called the Haygate. There's a wide-angled lens shot where you see PRENTICE walking up with the papers at the beginning, and it gives you the whole scope of how imposing these flats were.

As our luck would have it, the only uncooperative family on the Haygate Estate was in the flat upstairs from where we were filming. Every time we started to shoot, they would bang on their floor. It was an absolute nightmare and it was really putting the actors off their performance. I think we eventually had to pay the 'family from hell' off and put them up in a five-star hotel for the weekend. They were delighted.

Gemma Baker plays TRACEY, who the boys refer to as REENIE. Gemma's a great girl and a big Chelsea fan and nothing like her character in the film, of course! The reason they call her REENIE is because, back in the seventies and eighties, you would never really see girls at football. It was a rare sight. It's completely changed now, of course, but when these boys used to spot a girl walking out onto the terraces, they used to shout, "Reenie, Reenie!" Apparently there really was a Reenie, the daughter of a docker, who became the banter of the terraces. Not sure why though, but I can guess!

I love the newspapers in that scene and how the art department mocked them up. I never realised that the News of the World back in those days was broadsheet-size. Getting all those fine details right helps to sell the reality. JSB

Right, that's it. Newcastle away
next Saturday. We'll give the cunts
something to write about.

CASS walks to a cabinet and takes out a folder. He
opens it and we see that there are paper cuttings from
previous articles. They sit around the table and CASS
flicks through the pages. He finds a cutting regarding
a petrol bomb.

                    CASS (CONT'D)
          I want revenge from those cunts,
          for the petrol bomb they threw
          into our end last season.

                    FREEMAN
          I'm surprised they even have
          fucking petrol. Ain't it coal they
          use in their motors up there as
          well then?

                    PRENTICE
          I hate going up north though.
          What a poxy fucking shithole.

                    FREEMAN
          Especially Newcastle. I swear them
          Geordies are just jocks with the
          shit kicked out of them.

CASS flicks through the pages.

                    CASS
          Say what you want about them,
          they got fuck-all style but do they
          fucking hate cockneys! Even their
          shirters want to have it with yer.

>   FREEMAN
>   If they're wearing any. It needs
>   to be something different
>   though, Cass. They'll be waiting
>   for us coming off the train as
>   usual. It's not the best sight
>   when you have five or six
>   hundred mad Geordie lumps
>   waiting at the station for yer.

>   CASS
>   Alright, we'll put our fucking A-
>   team on them the night before the
>   game, when they ain't expecting it.

PRENTICE reveals business cards with, "Congratulations,
You've Just Met The ICF" written on them.

>   PRENTICE
>   Have a squint at them then.

CASS takes one.

>   CASS
>   Yeah, not bad mate!

>   FREEMAN
>   (sarcastically)
>   Ain't you going to put your name
>   and address on them as well then?

PRENTICE grabs it back and laughs.

>   PRENTICE
>   Cheeky bastard.

CASS turns to FREEMAN and picks up a newspaper.

CASS.
Nah mate, that's exactly what you
need if you want to let all these
cunts know who the top firm is.
A bit more fucking exposure.

FADE OUT.

INT. ANNE OF CLEVES PUB – DAY
CASS, FREEMAN and PRENTICE sit at a table beside
a news reporter. A camera crew are filming. The
PRESENTER addresses the camera lens.

PRESENTER
Welcome to *News Agenda*. Our
subject today is the 'English
Disease', football hooliganism. An

international poll recently claimed
that now, in 1983, after the Royal
Family it's what Britain is most
famous for. We've spoken to several
authorities from the world of
football, but today we're going to
talk to actual, real hooligans.
They've asked to remain nameless
but the gentlemen in question are
part of one of Britain's most
violent hooligan gangs, the Inter
City Force.

The PRESENTER turns to CASS, FREEMAN and
PRENTICE.*

> PRENTICE
> It's the Inter City Firm, love.

The PRESENTER smiles as if it makes no difference.

> PRESENTER
> Now you're real hooligans. Tell us
> what it's like.

The PRESENTER addresses CASS.

> PRESENTER (CONT'D)
> I'm intrigued to know why you in

---

* The TV PRESENTER was an actress called Lucy Russell, who plays her as naïve and
middleclass. We tried to show this by giving her ridiculous questions and her getting
the ICF's name wrong. She calls them the Inter City Force.

  The thing I most remember about that day was Stef, me and Cass sitting round the
monitor at the back of the pub. This was the day when Nonso really got the accent and
embodied the mannerisms of the real Cass. The day when everybody realised Nonso
was going to be phenomenal. .

  It's a really strong monologue and shows how the character of CASS is not an
inarticulate, one-dimensional hooligan. It says everything about those guys, about the
time period, what they thought about themselves and why they were doing what they
were doing. JSB

particular are so attracted to this
extremely violent way of life. Isn't
football the hotbed of racism we
always hear about?

INT. DOLL CHAMBERS' LIVING ROOM – NIGHT
The following week, DOLL and CECIL watch the TV in
despair at CASS's rant.

           CASS
           Maybe so, but it's the only place
           that I've ever been accepted.

CASS leans forward, not giving the PRESENTER time to
speak.

           CASS (CONT'D)
           This is the way I see it, right. Why
           did you invite me on this show?

CASS still doesn't give the PRESENTER time to reply.

CASS (CONT'D)
I'll tell you why. It's because the media in this country is obsessed with hooliganism. Most of it's sensationalised 'cos that's what sells papers. That's why you glamorise mobs like them train-smashing Chelsea lot. You have a lot to answer for, 'cos all you're doing right now with this programme is amplifying it, when you show the footage. You got to admit it, the middle class get a little thrill watching working-class men knocking seven barrels out of each other, from the safety of their own living rooms. We're not harming anyone else. We don't go around mugging old ladies or robbing for drugs or anything. It's just something for young men to do on a Saturday, to let off the steam they've built up during the week.

It ain't like we're real criminals or nothing. Some of my crew were in army fatigues in the Falklands not so long ago, and you lot called them heroes. We're a warring nation. It's built into males in this

country. We're born to fight.
There's three million unemployed
out there, with what to look
forward to? Everyone needs some
sort of buzz, don't they? Some
people do drugs, some are alkies,
some smoke sixty a day. Do you
think they're not a drain on the
NHS and the taxpayer?

As CASS stops speaking there is a stunned silence.

                    PRESENTER
                    Well, that's the informed view of
                    someone who has a clear notion of
                    why we have this problem. Let's
                    see what the other side had to say,
                    when I asked the Chief Inspector of
                    the Metropolitan Police last week.

FADE OUT

EXT. DOLL CHAMBERS' HOUSE – DAY
CASS walks up the front steps.

INT. DOLL CHAMBERS' LIVING ROOM – DAY
DOLL and CECIL are waiting for CASS. DOLL is agitated,
CECIL nervous. CASS enters.

                    CASS
                    Alright? Did you see me on TV last
                    week then?

                    DOLL
                    Yes, we saw you Cass, and so did
                    half of London, the phone hasn't
                    stopped ringing.

CASS
(cocky)
Yeah? Anybody else after an interview?

DOLL
(frustrated)
Do you honestly think the police ain't going to come after you and your silly little West Ham mates, now they seen you mouthing off on the television?

CASS
What you talking about? I never admitted to anything. Anyway, I got good money for that.

CECIL
Yeah, how much?

DOLL glares at CECIL.

DOLL
(angry)
Don't bloody encourage him!

DOLL turns on CASS.

DOLL (CONT'D)
You might as well paint a huge
target on your back, Cass. It's not as
if they're going to get you confused
with anyone, is it? You're setting
yourself up for a big fall, son.

CASS
(to Cecil)
Fifty quid.

CECIL
(impressed)
Fifty quid, eh?

DOLL
(snaps)
Cecil!

DOLL turns to CASS.

> DOLL (CONT'D)
> Well, was it worth it, or are you
> gonna tell me it's all for that
> overblown ego you seem to value
> so much nowadays?

> CASS
> Fifty quid I got! That's half a
> week's wages.

> DOLL
> Well, get saving son, because a
> good lawyer'll cost you a hell of a
> lot more than a piddling fifty quid.

CASS stares at DOLL.

> DOLL (CONT'D)
> I never brought you up to be a
> hooligan.

> CASS
> Nobody asked you to bring me up.

DOLL is hurt.

> DOLL
> Nobody asked me to bring you up
> either. I don't want you to waste
> your life, son.

There is a moment's silence.

> CASS
> I didn't mean to say that. You just
> don't understand what it's like for
> me, I'm not like you. I don't just
> want to be another worker bee. I
> ain't settling for that.

CASS points at CECIL.

> CASS (CONT'D)
> I ain't settling for a life like he's got.

DOLL is annoyed and also points at CECIL.

> DOLL
> Well he put a roof over your head
> and he put food on your table, and
> until you realise that that's what
> it takes to make you a man, you'll
> never be anybody.*

CASS stands in silence and looks at CECIL and DOLL,
then leaves the room.

ARCHIVE FOOTAGE OF PM MARGARET THATCHER
Thatcher's famous rant promising to rid the country of
hooliganism.

> THATCHER
> Everything but everything must
> be done, but in the end it comes to
> getting hold of the perpetrators of
> these terrible things.

---

* We were shooting in DOLL's house for about three or four days. It was really cramped
and it was towards the end of the shoot. Usually, at the end of a shoot everyone gets a
little bit edgy, as they're looking towards the finishing line. It's strange, because some
of the best performances in the film were on those days. JSB

EXT. ANNE OF CLEVES PUB – DAY

There are two vans parked outside the pub. CASS, FREEMAN and PRENTICE stand in front of FIFTY ICF members. They are selecting an ELITE ICF group. Each ICF member approaches individually, they open their jackets to show CASS a variety of violent weapons they've been carrying. CASS selects based on ferocity of weapon and individual.

> CASS
> Yes, yes, no, no, no, yes.

ARCHIVE FOOTAGE OF PM MARGARET THATCHER

> THATCHER
> That requires action by the
> Football Association, maybe that
> will require effective legislation.

EXT. ANNE OF CLEVES PUB – DAY

A YOUNG ICF MEMBER, who is 14 years old, approaches CASS.

> CASS
> (laughs)
> Behave son, we ain't Crystal
> fucking Palace.

> YOUNG ICF MEMBER
> (defensive)
> What?

> CASS
> (sympathetic)
> Maybe in a couple of years, eh?

The YOUNG ICF MEMBER pulls out a huge knife.

> YOUNG ICF MEMBER
> I fucking hate them Geordie cunts
> though, Cass. I'll cut them to fuck.

CASS shakes his head as the YOUNG ICF MEMBER walks
off, disappointed.

> CASS
> (astonished)
> Fuck me. That knife was almost as
> big as him!

CASS goes back to selecting his troops.

> CASS (CONT'D)
> No, no, no, yes.

ARCHIVE FOOTAGE OF PM MARGARET THATCHER

> THATCHER
> You will get the full cooperation
> of the police, and it requires the
> full cooperation of the people in
> those clubs because they know
> who are their supporters and
> who are not.

EXT. THE ROAD NORTH – EVENING
The two vans travel along a country road north. A sign
reads, "Newcastle 20 miles."

> FREEMAN (O.S.)
> (singing)
> Johnny Lyle's claret and blue
> army!

The ICF join in.

>   ICF ELITE (O.S.)
>   (singing)
>   Johnny Lyle's claret and blue
>   army! Johnny Lyle's claret and
>   blue army!

The ELITE thump the side of the van.

>   ICF ELITE (O.S.) (CONT'D)
>   (singing)
>   ICF, ICF, ICF!

INT. TRANSIT VAN – EVENING
In the back of the van, the ICF ELITE are packed in like
sardines.

>   ICF ELITE
>   (singing)
>   I'm forever blowing bubbles, pretty
>   bubbles in the air. They fly so high,
>   they reach the sky and like my
>   dreams they fade and die. Geordie's
>   always hiding, Millwall hiding too,
>   West Ham's always running, 'cos
>   we're running after you. United!
>   United!

They all laugh arrogantly.

>   ICF ELITE (CONT'D)
>   (shouting)
>   Aaaaaaaaaaaaaaaaaaaaaa!

ARCHIVE FOOTAGE OF PM MARGARET THATCHER

> THATCHER
> I want to get those people
> responsible, get them before a
> court and stiff sentences. So they
> will stop anyone else in their
> tracks from doing this.

INT. NEWCASTLE WORKING MEN'S CLUB – NIGHT
It's a stag party. There is a STRIPPER performing on stage and the pub is full of Newcastle Fans, the GEORDIES. They are in high spirits and singing the stripper song.

> GEORDIES
> (singing)
> Dada da, da dada da . . .

INT. TRANSIT VAN – EVENING
The singing is continued from inside the club.

GEORDIES (O.S.)
(singing)
'Way the lads, you should've seen
them ganin. Ganin alang the
Scotswood Road just as they were
standin'. All the lads and lasses,
smiles upon their faces, ganin
alang the Scotswood roaaaaaaaad!
To see the bladen races.

The ELITE ICF all start grinning nervously.

FREEMAN
(quietly)
Dirty northern bastards!

CASS
It's time to make a real name for
ourselves, boys, and show every
other fucking mob in Britain who

the real fucking daddies are. You
fucking with me, or what?

The ELITE are wide-eyed with adrenalin and buzzing.

INT. NEWCASTLE WORKING MEN'S CLUB – EVENING
As the STRIPPER finishes her routine, a NORTHERN
COMIC arrives on the stage. He turns to the STRIPPER
as she exits.

> NORTHERN COMIC
> The lovely Deborah there. I'd pay
> for that, I would like.

The GEORDIES laugh. The NORTHERN COMIC itches at his crotch and pretends to wince as if he's caught some STD.

> NORTHERN COMIC (CONT'D)
> Just like I paid for it with her
> mother.

THE GEORDIES cheer.

> NORTHERN COMIC (CONT'D)
> Alright then, there were these two
> Pakis . . .

EXT. NEWCASTLE WORKING MEN'S CLUB – NIGHT
The vans are parked outside.

INT. TRANSIT VAN – NIGHT
CASS addresses the troops. He is bursting with energy and very animated.

CASS
We know who their top boys are,
right, so we've got to deal with
them first and the rest will
fucking crumble. But these cunts
don't fuck about, yeah, you saw
that last season. Everybody's got
to stick together, because any one
of us goes down for this lot, we all
go down. This is the big one, yeah.
There'll be no more talk after this
on who's the number one fucking
firm. Come on West Ham, let's go
fucking mental!

INT. NEWCASTLE WORKING MENS CLUB – NIGHT
The NORTHERN COMIC is about to start another joke
when we hear the door swing open, interrupting him.
The pub goes silent. The NORTHERN COMIC looks
towards the back of the audience at the door.

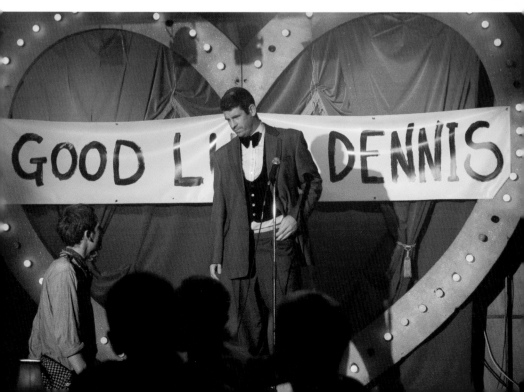

NORTHERN COMIC
(sarcastically)
Sit down then, Kunta Kinte, and if
Chicken George is walking in behind
yer, tell him to shut his gob 'n' all.*

The GEORDIES turn and we see CASS standing at the
door with FREEMAN, PRENTICE and the ELITE ICF. It
takes a second before the GEORDIES register that it's
the ICF.

GEORDIE 1
(shouts)
Fucking cockney bastards!

The GEORDIES arm themselves with bottles, glasses,
chairs, tables and ashtrays. CASS unveils a huge sword
from his coat. The ELITE unveil their weapons and let
loose. They charge into the GEORDIES, stabbing and
squirting. It's like a Wild West brawl. The tables, chairs,
glasses and ashtrays are used by the GEORDIES in
defence.

FADE TO BLACK

INT. PRISON, CORRIDOR – DAY
CASS is escorted by a PRISON GUARD. We hear the
JUDGE sentencing him.

---

* The guy who played the NORTHERN COMIC is called Dan Skinner. He's actually from
Wimbledon, but his accent is brilliant. I asked him, "How long did it take to get that
accent perfected?" He said, "Well, I used to share a flat with a guy from
Middlesbrough." He then said, "What kind of routine are we going to do?" I said, "It's
got to be really harsh, it's got to be really eighties and un-PC and as Bernard Manning
as you can get." Dan was really nervous about some of the jokes, but when he did his
routine he went so far over the top that we had to cut the worst of it out! He did really
well though, and he was so, so convincing you'd never think he was a Surrey boy.
    The crowd in this scene was made up of extras from all over the country. There were
my in-laws, my mates from Aberdeen, some Newcastle lads, Middlesbrough lads,
Hartlepool, Sheffield Wednesday and guys from Nottingham Forest. You'll even see a
cameo by Frank McAvennie, smashing a bottle over FREEMAN's head! JSB

JUDGE (O.S.)
Carol Lindo Powell Pennant ... You
have been found guilty of the
charges brought by this court, and
it is now my duty to pass sentence.
You are an extremely dangerous
hooligan and a scourge of society.
Let this sentence serve as an
example and deterrent to any
likeminded thug, that the justice
system will no longer tolerate your
despicable behaviour. You will
serve a period of four years.

As CASS reaches the end of the corridor he is led
through a gate. After he passes through the gate, it
slams loudly behind him.

INT. PRISON, CLOTHES ALLOCATION ROOM – DAY
CASS queues behind a black prisoner, DELROY, and a
white prisoner, HARRY. Behind the counter is a
Prison Guard, RON, who has two piles of clothes, one
good, one shabby.

RON
Name?

DELROY
Jackson.

RON looks at a list then dumps some shabby clothes on the counter. DELROY is unimpressed and grabs the clothes.

DELROY (CONT'D)
Fucking screw bastard.

RON looks at DELROY as he walks off.

RON
(sarcastically)
Welcome home, son.

HARRY approaches RON.

RON (CONT'D)
(smiling)
Alright, Harry?

HARRY
Ron.

RON
What you in for this time then?

HARRY
Getting caught, mate.

They laugh. RON gives HARRY new clothes of decent quality.

HARRY (CONT'D)
Cheers.

CASS approaches RON, whose expression changes back to a scowl. CASS points to the good clothes pile.

CASS
Extra large, mate.

RON gives him the shabby clothes. CASS pushes them back across the counter to RON.

CASS (CONT'D)
(sarcastically)
No thanks, I'll have the Lacoste ones, pal.

RON leans forward and whispers to CASS.

RON
No you fucking won't, you cheeky bastard. You'll have the ones I decide you're having.

CASS holds in his anger, then smiles.

CASS
Listen, mate. If I was doing your job, I'd be a miserable old cunt as

well. But look at it this way, at
least you get to have a shower
with a fucking bird.

RON is taken by surprise. He pauses, then chuckles.

> RON
> Fucking hell, you ain't seen my
> missus, mate. You'd never get that
> fat old cunt in the shower when
> I'm in it.

RON is really pleased with his joke and laughs for an
uncomfortably long time.*

> RON (CONT'D)
> (still laughing)
> Name?

> CASS
> Pennant.

RON immediately stops laughing. He recognises the name.

> RON
> Ah! You're that hooligan on the
> news! I used to go and see QPR
> back in the day. It was always you
> or Millwall, that was the number
> one firm back in the day.

---

* A lot of the extras in the prison clothes allocation room scene were the big names of
the hooligan eras of the seventies and eighties: Bill Gardner, Brett and co from the ICF,
guys from the Blades Business Crew, Villa's C-Crew and Birmingham's Zulus, it was
like a Who's Who of that world.
    Eddie Webber, who plays PRISON GUARD RON, was quite nervous as he's a Millwall
fan. The original line in the script was supposed to be, "You'd never get the fat old cow
in the shower when I'm in it." But Eddie said, "No, no, it's got to be harder than that.
It's got to be, 'You'd never get the fat old cunt in the shower.'" It's one of the funniest
lines in the film and always gets a big laugh! JSB

RON puts the shabby clothing back and gives CASS some quality stuff. CASS looks shocked by the attention as he walks off.

> RON (CONT'D)
> (calling after him)
> Come on then, who's the best mob
> you went up against? Eh?

CASS does not respond and walks off. RON shrugs and turns to the next PRISONER.

> RON (CONT'D)
> Next.

INT. ZULU'S PRISON CELL – DAY
ZULU, a powerful looking black prisoner, and a skinny black prisoner, KID, lie on their bunks in a squalid cell.

> ZULU
> Hey dread, gimme some draw. I need
> a draw. You no give me you fuckery
> guy, it's me you deal with, blood.

KID is terrified. The door opens and CASS walks in. The door then shuts firmly behind him. CASS surveys the dreadful conditions in the cell.

> CASS
> (sarcastically)
> Fuck me, have a word. They never
> said it was a five-star gaff.

CASS looks at ZULU, who stares back menacingly.

> CASS (CONT'D)
> Alright, mate?

ZULU does not reply and continues to stare. CASS walks to the spare bunk. The mattress is torn and looks like a piece of cheese.

> CASS (CONT'D)
> I suppose I get to sleep on this bit
> of fucking cheddar then.

ZULU sucks his teeth in disrespect. CASS starts to get annoyed as he lies on his bunk. ZULU jumps off his bunk

and walks around the cell like a peacock. ZULU starts to light matches and throw them at KID. KID is crying.

> CASS (CONT'D)
> (diplomatically)
> Leave it out, mate.

ZULU is annoyed at CASS's cockney accent and turns sharply.

> ZULU
> What you saying there, choc-ice?*

---

*The ZULU scene was pretty much word-for-word how it happened in real life. CASS is victimised by a black person this time for being 'white'. I think that's really important, to show the racism from the other side too, to show how he's an outsider in the black community as well.

That to me was the best scene in prison, because it had a lot of action and sharp dialogue. We went into the sound postproduction and put on lots of effects: doors clanging, prisoners shouting in the background, pipes being banged – everything that Cass had described as to how prison life actually was. JSB

CASS
You what, mate?

ZULU sucks his teeth in a mark of disrespect.

ZULU
You're not brethren. You don't talk
to me, raasclaat. You talk like the
white man.

CASS speaks to ZULU in broken English like a tourist,
pointing to himself, then at ZULU.

CASS
(sarcastic)
Sorry, me no understand you.

ZULU approaches CASS.

ZULU
(shouts)
You're not a real black man!

CASS explodes. He rubs the skin on his arms vigorously
as if to state how deep the colour is.

CASS
(shouts)
Black!? Not fucking really black!?
What the fuck's that then, yer
cunt!?

ZULU walks around the cell, pumping his fist and
animated.

ZULU
Black power going to deal with the

white devil. Going to deal with all
the Uncle Tom collaborators.

CASS
You been watching too much
American TV. This is Britain, mate.

ZULU spits on the floor.

ZULU
Imperialist, colonial oppression.
The black man is going to rise up
and go back to Africa. One nation,
Haile Selassie, kill the Babylon.
Rastafari!

CASS
(angrily)
Best leave your BMW and gold
chains behind when you go, mate.
There's not much use for them in a
mud hut.

ZULU comes for CASS. They are both huge men. KID
turns on his side to face the wall.

ZULU
You're bloodclaat.

CASS continues to stare at ZULU.

CASS
(angrily)
Anyway, I thought Jamaicans and
Africans fucking hated each other?
Go on back to Africa then, you cunt,
where black man is killing black

man, and take that chip on your
shoulder with yer. There'll be no
playing the rude boy at nightclubs
and screwing pretty white pussy
there though, you racist mug cunt.

ZULU drops his gaze for a second, then attacks him.
They fight viciously. There is loud banging as the
PRISONERS scream and bang the pipes in their cells.
CASS smashes ZULU's head into the door. ZULU bites
CASS's leg. CASS pushes the alarm button. Both men
are badly beaten. ZULU picks up a razorblade and
waves it at CASS.

> CASS
> (breathless)
> Come on then. You better fucking
> splice me, you cunt, 'cos if you
> don't I ain't stopping.

Suddenly, ZULU drops the razorblade and walks past
CASS as if nothing has happened. ZULU climbs on the
top bunk, rolls over and mutters under his breath.

> ZULU
> He's not a black man. I won't share
> no cell with no white trash
> hooligan.

CASS is shocked at the sudden end to hostilities.

> CASS
> (out of breath)
> Fucking mad cunt.

FADE OUT

INT. PRISON CORRIDOR – NIGHT
The corridor is quiet. A PRISON GUARD reads a newspaper.

INT. MARLON'S PRISON CELL – NIGHT
CASS has been moved into a new cell with MARLON, a good-looking black prisoner, who is smoking a joint. MARLON wears a pair of distinctive spectacles. CASS is bruised from the fight.

>   MARLON
>   You missing your Rasta boyfriend
>   then?

>   CASS
>   I'll get over it. We promised to keep
>   in touch though.

MARLON laughs and offers the joint to CASS.

>   CASS (CONT'D)
>   Cheers.

CASS puffs then splutters. MARLON hands CASS the utensils.

>   MARLON
>   New boy always rolls.

CASS stares at the rolling papers.

>   MARLON (CONT'D)
>   Problem?

>   CASS
>   (embarrassed)
>   Sorry mate, I don't know how.

MARLON laughs.

> MARLON
> In all my years in nick, I never met
> a black man who couldn't skin up.
> This ain't cool, Mr Hooligan. You're
> a disgrace to the brothers.

CASS laughs.

> CASS
> I know mate, and it gets worse. I
> can't dance either.

They laugh and are both stoned. It breaks the ice.

> MARLON
> Where the fuck you from, man,
> Mars or something?

CASS shrugs.

> CASS
> It fucking felt a bit like it as a kid,
> mate. Got adopted, didn't I?

> MARLON
> Who by, the Ku Klux Klan?

They laugh. There is silence for a while.

> CASS
> I hate all that racist bollocks.

> MARLON
> The screws been at you already, eh?

CASS
Nah mate, I ain't just talking about
from white to black. It's just as
fucking bad the other way round!

MARLON
You had a look in the mirror
recently to check which colour you
are, Hooligan?

CASS
I ain't no fucking Uncle Tom,
right? I bet I've had more stick for
being black than you ever fucking
have, mate.

MARLON
Chill, chill out, Hooligan.

CASS
Look, mate. My mum was a fifty-
year-old white woman when she
got me from that orphanage. They
never gave her a fucking
instruction manual on how to
raise a black kid. How the fuck
was she meant to know all that
stuff about plaiting your hair up
or moisturising your skin?

MARLON shrugs.

CASS (CONT'D)
My face used to look like a fucking
bombsite when I first started
shaving, and I could just imagine
old Doll Chambers trying to look
after her little boy's new afro!

MARLON laughs.

>MARLON
>I never thought about it that way.

>CASS
>I did, mate. Every fucking day!

MARLON contemplates.

>MARLON
>You need to write all that shit
>down.

CASS thinks.

>CASS
>Kill the time, I suppose. It was the
>only fucking thing I was any good
>at, at school anyway, mate.

>MARLON
>You went to school then?

>CASS
>Cheeky cunt. You can talk, look at
>the fucking state of yer with them
>glasses. You win them in a raffle or
>something, did yer?

>MARLON
>You got a lot to learn, Hooligan.

>CASS
>What, from you?

MARLON
Listen, Hooligan. You come in here
and they take everything away
from you, right. You're nothing in
here. When they give you that
number and brand you with Her
Majesty's cattle prod, how the fuck
do you separate yourself from the
rest of the herd?

MARLON takes off his spectacles and points to them.

MARLON (CONT'D)
That's how. You got to keep your
own identity in here or you're
never going to get through it. You'll
find out, Hooligan. You need to do
anything you can do to keep your
dignity in here, to stop them from
turning you into an animal, like
most of them are in this place.

CASS shrugs.

MARLON (CONT'D)
So you're the top man in your
world then?

CASS
(defensive)
One of them. Why?

MARLON
Well, leave that at the door, mate.
You see yourself as the big cheese
'cos that's how your football lot
treat you. But when they ain't

around you'll soon feel like you're
just another two-bit black con to
the cunts in here.

CASS
I don't know who the cunts are,
mate. The fucking screws think I'm
a schwarz and the Rastas think
I'm a fucking coconut.

MARLON laughs.

MARLON
You're a bit unique, ain't yer,
Hooligan?

They laugh. MARLON says something in Jamaican
patois. CASS looks confused and doesn't react.

MARLON (CONT'D)
(laughs)
You don't understand patois then?

CASS
Yeah, just like you don't
understand Japanese, mate. Why
d'you still speak that bollocks,
anyway?

MARLON
It's my heritage, man. I only really
speak it with my mother, or in
here to piss the screws off.

CASS shrugs.

MARLON (CONT'D)
You still got a lot to learn about
your culture, Hooligan.

CASS thinks.

CASS
The only culture I have, mate, is
West Ham fucking United!

There is a sound of keys turning in the door. A
PRISON GUARD enters. CASS and MARLON look
confused.

MARLON
(disrespectfully)
What?

The PRISON GUARD looks at MARLON, but points at
CASS.

PRISON GUARD
Somebody wants a word with the
hooligan.

CASS looks at MARLON for reassurance, but MARLON
shrugs.

INT. PRISON CORRIDOR – NIGHT
CASS has a confused expression as he walks in front of
the PRISON GUARD.

CASS
(on edge)
What the fuck is this all about? I
ain't done nothing.

The PRISON GUARD remains silent and stops outside a cell.

INT. RAY'S CELL – NIGHT
From inside the cell, we hear keys going into the lock and the door opens. The PRISON GUARD motions for CASS to enter. CASS enters hesitantly and it takes a moment for him to register the familiar face of RAY. CASS's expression changes to a smile.

>CASS
>Fuck me!

The door shuts behind him. RAY's is no ordinary cell. It's obvious he has major influence in prison.

>CASS (CONT'D)
>I thought you were in
>Wandsworth?

>RAY
>I am sometimes, but the cunts
>keep you on the move so you don't
>get too fucking comfy.

CASS looks round at the single cell. It has lots of boxing memorabilia on the walls.

>CASS
>Doesn't seem to have taken you
>too long to get your feet under the
>table in here, though.

>RAY
>You can talk, you cunt. All over the
>papers and the news. What you
>then, the world's first celebrity
>football thug?

CASS smiles. RAY is curious.

> RAY (CONT'D)
> How you settling in, mate?

CASS shakes his head.

> CASS
> Ah, don't.

> RAY
> It takes a while, mate. Your first
> month is the worst, I always reckon.

> CASS
> It couldn't have gotten off to a
> better start.

> RAY
> Yeah, I heard about the rumble in
> the jungle.

> CASS
> Fucking mental, mate.

RAY laughs.

> RAY
> How long did they give you then?

> CASS
> Four year.

RAY shakes his head.

> RAY
> Fuck me. Four year just for
> fighting over a poxy football team?

CASS doesn't realise it's a criticism.

>   CASS
>   I know. It weren't even at the game
>   either. Fucking liberty, mate!

RAY shrugs.

>   RAY
>   You'll be out in two. Anyway, listen,
>   mate.

RAY leans forward as he gets to the point.

>   RAY (CONT'D)
>   You were knocking about with
>   them two little artful dodgers the
>   last time I saw yer. What's all this
>   about an Inter City Firm? What
>   happened to the old Southbank or
>   the TBF from Mile End?

>   CASS
>   What d'you mean?

>   RAY
>   (sarcastic)
>   What do I mean? I mean, tell me
>   about how your mob operates?
>   Where's the money in it? Who's
>   the guv'nor?

>   CASS
>   There's no real guv'nor, mate. There's
>   a few of us who organise it and
>   there's a few little firms who come
>   together under one big banner.

RAY
But where's the money come
from? Protection or something?

CASS
Nah, there ain't no money in it.

CASS smiles.

CASS CONT'D
Unless you count the under-fives
taxing some cunt for his Burberry.

RAY
(confused)
No fucking money. You mugging
me off?

CASS
It's all about the buzz. It ain't
about business, it ain't that kind
of firm.

RAY
(laughs)
The buzz? The fucking buzz? Why
the fuck go to all the bother if
there's nothing in it for yer?
Bunch of fucking schoolkids if you
ask me, Cass.

CASS shrugs.

RAY (CONT'D)
(curious)
How many bodies can you pull
together then?

> CASS
> Depends on what's going on, but
> anything from nifty to a carpet and
> that's hardcore, no hangers-on.
> Another couple of ton if it's a big 'un.

> RAY
> (impressed)
> That ain't bad, mate. You some sort
> of black hooligan Pope or
> something now then, Cass? The
> pied piper of Plaistow.

CASS laughs.

> RAY (CONT'D)
> I might have a bit of work for you
> on the out Cass, it so happens, if
> that's the kind of numbers you can
> pull together.

> CASS
> (serious)
> Cheers for the offer, but I ain't into
> anything criminal, mate.

RAY stares at him then bursts out laughing. CASS doesn't see the irony.

> RAY
> What the fuck you doing in here
> then, you silly bastard? Anyway,
> who said anything about being
> criminal, you cheeky fucker?

RAY stands up and walks to the door. He knocks on it and we hear the keys turning in the lock. He turns to CASS and winks.

RAY (CONT'D)
Go on then mate, fuck off.

CASS smiles, then goes to leave.

FADE OUT.

INT. MARLON'S CELL – NIGHT
1985
MUSIC – LAND OF HOPE AND GLORY
There's obviously been a time shift, as CASS now has a
moustache. He is writing on prison headed paper. There
is a big pile of similar sheets at the end of his bed.
MARLON lies there smoking, staring at the ceiling.

> CASS (V.O.)
> During the whole of my sentence,
> nothing moved in or out of nick
> without Ray's blessing. It was like
> having a prison governor who wore
> a con's uniform, so pens, paper
> and privileges were never in short
> supply. You can get through a lot
> of trees in two years on twenty-
> three-hour bang-up. You gotta do
> something 'cos if you wish your
> time away a minute's not like an
> hour, it's like a week.

ARCHIVE FOOTAGE MONTAGE
Footage from the era of the miners' strike, the Heysel
disaster and the Luton v Millwall riot.

> CASS (V.O.)
> The Tories had smashed the fuck
> out of the miners with the biggest
> group of uniformed thugs the

country had ever seen and, after
the Heysel Stadium disaster, even
the IRA were higher in the
popularity poles than us hooligans.
Thatcher's firm had seriously
mobbed up against anyone who
mixed their football with their
violence.

INT. MARLON'S CELL – NIGHT

CASS is writing. MARLON is
reading some of CASS's pages.

MARLON
(impressed)
This lot can't all be fucking true,
Cass.

CASS
(smiles)
Fuck off. Every fucking word, mate.

MARLON
It ain't half bad, you know.

CASS doesn't look up and continues to write.

MARLON (CONT'D)
Where were your family from,
then?

CASS continues to write.

CASS
Both from somewhere in London,
not sure exactly where.

MARLON laughs.

> MARLON
> No man, your real family.

CASS stops writing.

> CASS
> What you mean? They are my real
> family. They're the only ones that
> ever wanted me.

> MARLON
> You never try and find your other
> ones though?

> CASS
> (dismissive)
> Ain't interested, mate. What good
> would that do me?

MARLON sits up on his bed.

> MARLON
> Don't take this the wrong way, but
> I reckon that's your biggest
> problem, man.

> CASS
> Don't take this the wrong way
> either, mate. Fuck off.

MARLON laughs.

> MARLON
> If you don't know who your father
> was and you don't know who your

grandfather was, how the fuck you
supposed to know where your
roots are? Who you are?

            CASS
            (defensive)
Who the fuck are you, Mother
Teresa? What the fuck would a
petty criminal like you know about
stuff like that anyway? If you had
any brains you certainly wouldn't
be in here.

            MARLON
            (philosophical)
You might be right, mate, but if
there's one thing this place gives
you, it's plenty time to think.

INT. PRISON, DISCHARGING ROOM – DAY
CASS carries his makeshift book of pages under his
arm and waits to collect his belongings from a prison
guard, SERGEANT MULLINS. MULLINS gives CASS his
belongings, but notices the paper he's carrying.

            SERGEANT MULLINS
Whoa, whoa, whoa, what's that?

            CASS
Just some stuff I've been
scribbling down.

MULLINS reaches out, ordering CASS to hand it over.

            SERGEANT MULLINS
Give us it here.

CASS reluctantly hands it over. MULLINS flicks through the pages.

> SERGEANT MULLINS (CONT'D)
> Prison rule 12786 states, "Inmates are not permitted to be discharged with any possession they did not enter the prison with."

> CASS
> (frustrated)
> Ah, come on mate!

MULLINS looks at CASS with contempt.

> SERGEANT MULLINS
> (sneers)
> I certainly am not your mate.

CASS tries to reason with him.

> CASS
> (pleads)
> I've been writing that for ages.
> That's my life in there.

MULLINS points to the HMP royal crest stamp on the paper.

> SERGEANT MULLINS
> What does that say, sonny?

> CASS
> (subdued)
> Her Majesty's Prison.

SERGEANT MULLINS
(condescending)
Exactly. Property of Her Majesty,
not . . .

MULLINS looks at the discharge papers for CASS's
name and laughs when he finds it.

SERGEANT MULLINS (CONT'D)
(mocks)
. . . Carol Pennant.

CASS is about to lunge at MULLINS, who invites him on.

SERGEANT MULLINS (CONT'D)
Come on then. Let's see if we can
find out if you fight like a girl as
well, Carol. 'Cos if we do, you'll be
walking straight down that fucking
corridor and back into the cosy
little cave you just crawled out of.

MULLINS throws the paper in the bin. CASS grits his
teeth.

CASS
That's my future you've just slung
away.

SERGEANT MULLINS
Future? Tell me, what fucking
future is there exactly for a two-bit
schwarzer football hooligan like
you?

CASS inhales deeply, puffs out his chest and walks
away.

SERGEANT MULLINS (CONT'D)
(calling after him)
Hope to see you back here soon . . .
Carol.*

FADE OUT

INT. THE ANNE OF CLEVES PUB – DAY
A live band, THE COCKNEY REJECTS, play in the bar, which is full of familiar ICF faces and 'Welcome Home' banners. Two girls, ELAINE and LINDA, sit at the bar. There are also a group of National Front (NF) SKINHEADS in the corner.

ELAINE
I don't know why I ever agreed to come here. My dad'd kill me if he knew I was coming to some football thug's party. Sorry Linda, I ain't waiting here all day, just to cheer on some released convict.

ELAINE gets up to leave.

---

* The actor who's playing the prison guard SERGEANT MULLINS is Ralph Ineson. People will recognise Ralph as FINCHY from The Office. I'd worked with Ralph before and always had him in mind for that part. The scene signifies CASS getting his life taken away from him. Throwing the books in the bin has a huge effect on his state of mind and throws him back into the arms of the ICF. JSB

LINDA
(pleads)
Come on Elaine, he's West Ham.

ELAINE
(laughs)
And what? You think I give a shit
about your crappy little football
team?

LINDA smiles and gives her the finger.

LINDA
Too late anyway, here he is.*

We see CASS walking through the doors with a swagger.
ELAINE sees CASS and is impressed, but tries to hide it.

ELAINE
Is that him? Who, that cocky
looking sod? Jesus!

There is a loud cheer. CASS takes the applause.
FREEMAN and PRENTICE are first to welcome him back.

FREEMAN/PRENTICE
Speech! Speech!

The pub quietens. CASS catches ELAINE's eye. She
looks away.

---

* It was really important for the female characters to be as strong as the male ones.
That's really why we picked Nathalie [ELAINE] and Lorraine [LINDA], because of
Natalie's performance in My Summer of Love and Lorraine's in London to Brighton,
two really strong independent British films.

I enjoy watching the 'Welcome Home' scene as it has a huge Union Jack in the
background which really gives that period feel. You never really see the Union Jack
that much these days, unless it's at the Olympics or some royal event. It really gives
you that eighties feel.

We used some artistic licence here because it was an easier way of fitting it into the
storyline. It wasn't exactly how the real Cass and Elaine met. JSB

CASS
(slightly embarrassed)
Don't know what to say really.

PRENTICE
That's a fucking first then.

Everyone laughs.

CASS
(smiles)
Glad to see you ain't lost it, mate.

FREEMAN
Can't lose it if you never had it!

EVERYONE laughs again. CASS looks towards ELAINE,
who looks away shyly.

CASS

I'd just like to say thanks to
everyone for coming here tonight
and for coming to visit me inside.
When you're in there even stupid
little things like a postcard or
something can keep you going, so
for any one of you that wrote, and
I know most of you can't . . .

They all laugh

CASS (CONT'D)
. . . I won't forget it. That's about it
really. Who we got Saturday then?

The band starts to play again. CASS leaves the stage to
shake hands with people. He catches ELAINE'S eye again.
There is an attraction building.

EXT. THE ANNE OF CLEVES PUB – NIGHT
It's been several hours since the party started, and we
see through the window that it's now in full swing with
the band playing.

INT. THE ANNE OF CLEVES PUB – NIGHT
The band have stopped. ELAINE is still sitting at the
bar with LINDA, who is ordering a drink. SHAUN, an NF
skinhead, approaches and stands next to LINDA. CASS
chats to PRENTICE but is distracted as he and ELAINE
exchange glances.

FREEMAN is with some ICF. They are snorting cocaine.
FREEMAN approaches ELAINE with a swagger.

> FREEMAN
> Alright, sexy?

> ELAINE
> (dismissive)
> Alright?

                    FREEMAN
                    You on your own then, darling?

                    ELAINE
                    Yeah, you know how it is, I'm sure.

                    FREEMAN
                    You want to come and join me and
                    the boys to powder your nose?

FREEMAN motions doing a line of cocaine and turns to
the ICF for acknowledgement. They laugh and encourage
him.

                    ELAINE
                    (sarcastically)
                    Sorry, but I don't use that stuff. I
                    already have a personality, thank
                    you.

ELAINE stands up to walk away.

                    FREEMAN
                    You off then, darling?

ELAINE doesn't make eye contact with FREEMAN as
she walks past him towards the toilets.

                    ELAINE
                    Yes love, I need a little breather.
                    You got me all flushed, darling!

LINDA suddenly gets up off her barstool.

                    LINDA
                    (shouts)
                    Oi, you dirty little cunt.

ELAINE runs back to her. SHAUN is laughing.

    ELAINE
    What's wrong?

    LINDA
    Cheeky bastard's just tried to stick
    his hand in my knickers.

    ELAINE
    Wanker!

    SHAUN
    (laughs)

Calm down, Treacle, I was only messing about. Anyway,
you looked as though you were up for it.

LINDA throws her drink over SHAUN. EVERYONE
laughs, but SHAUN is humiliated. He pushes LINDA,
who falls over, banging her head on the bar.

> ELAINE
> (screams)
> You fucking prick. Who the fuck
> d'you think you are?

CASS walks over and turns to SHAUN. The bar goes quiet.

> CASS
> (calmly)
> Probably best you fuck off home,
> mate.

SHAUN's face contorts in rage. FREEMAN and PRENTICE
square up to the NF group.

SHAUN
Home? Fuck off home? This is my
fucking home, mate. Where exactly
would you say yours was, eh?

CASS is about to snap but resists.

CASS
Alright mate, no problem. I don't
want any trouble, OK?

SHAUN smirks when he sees CASS has backed down
and returns to his NF SKINHEAD group. ELAINE helps
LINDA to her feet.*

---

* It was really important to show that, although CASS was accepted by the majority of
the East End, there was still obviously that Far Right element who wouldn't accept a
black man. Johnny Palmiero, who plays the SKINHEAD, gives a fantastic performance
– really convincing and very nasty. When we shot the scene where LINDA slaps him,
Lorraine hit Johnny so hard that she knocked him off his feet. The whole place just
took this massive gasp but Johnny never batted an eyelid and continued in character.
   One extra, who will remain nameless, liked to be in the forefront of things so we
called him 'Camera Shy'. On one of the takes, when LINDA gets thrown to the ground
by the SKINHEAD, 'Camera Shy' ran from the other end of the pub into the shot,
grabbed Johnny and said, "You can't do that, you can't hit a girl!" He was either drunk
or he was just getting carried away with the whole affair! It was a really funny
moment, looking back on it, but it didn't feel funny at the time because he ruined the
take. Cass had to take him outside to give him a talking to! JSB

LINDA
Ain't you going to do him then? I
thought you were the tough guy?

CASS is slightly embarrassed and looks at ELAINE,
who smiles back.

CASS
He ain't really worth it, girl.

CASS puts his hand out to shake ELAINE's hand.

> CASS (CONT'D)
> I'm Cass.

ELAINE gives him a coy smile.

> ELAINE
> (cheekily)
> Are yer?

They continue to shake hands as they stare at each other. It's happening.

INT. DOLL CHAMBERS' LIVING ROOM – EVENING

CECIL and DOLL wait nervously, glancing at the clock. DOLL is beginning to look frail. We hear the front door opening.

> CECIL
> (anxiously)
> Remember Doll, you promised.

DOLL scowls at CECIL. The door opens and CASS swaggers in.

                    CASS
                    (cocky)
                    What's for dinner then, Mum, you
                    done my favourite have yer?

DOLL smiles nervously.

                    DOLL
                    Hello son, welcome home.

DOLL gives CASS an awkward hug.

                    DOLL CONT'D
                    Of course I done your favourite.

INT. DOLL CHAMBERS' DINING ROOM – NIGHT
DOLL, CASS and CECIL sit round the table. CASS devours
the food.

DOLL
Didn't they feed you in there
then?

CASS looks up and smiles.

CASS
I ain't saying the food was bad,
but they had me cooking it half the
time.

They all laugh.

CECIL
(intrigued)
So, what was it like then?

CASS
(shrugs)
Alright, I suppose. I won't be
rebooking for next year though.

CECIL laughs but DOLL sighs. CASS looks at her to see
what's wrong.

DOLL
You need to get a job now, son, and
keep your head down for a while.

CASS
(laughs)
Gimme a break, I only got out
yesterday!

DOLL
Well I just hope you learnt your
lesson!

CASS
(dismissive)
Learnt my lesson? What you
talking about?

DOLL
Don't try and make out you're an
angel, son. It was only a matter of
time before you got put away for
something or other.

There is silence. CASS gets up to leave.

DOLL (CONT'D)
Where d'you think you're
going now?

CASS
Don't you ever give it a rest?

DOLL
(pleads)
They're saying they're going to
make a real example of you
football louts, after those poor
Italians got killed at that game in
Belgium. Is that what you want?

CASS shrugs and is about to leave the room. CECIL
stands up, out of the blue.

CECIL
(blurts it out)
It's about time you told him, Doll.

DOLL turns away.

CASS
Told me what, Mum?

DOLL cannot face him.

CECIL
You've got to tell him, Doll!

CASS
What?

DOLL
(reluctantly)
They're trying to contact you.

CASS
(confused)
Who?

DOLL
Them that gave you away. They've
been writing letters to you
through Dr Barnardo's.

CASS is stunned as CECIL shows him some unopened
letters with the Dr Barnardo's logo.

CASS
Well, fuck them!

CECIL
Language, son, not in front of your
mother. Don't you want to open
them then?

CASS
Nah. I don't want anything to do
with them. You two are my family.

DOLL cuddles CASS in relief.

>CECIL
>Are you sure?

DOLL turns sharply and stares at CECIL.

>DOLL
>Would you just shut up, Cecil! You
>heard him, he doesn't want to
>know. We're his family, not them.

>DOLL (CONT'D)
>You need to settle down, meet a
>girl, have a family of your own, son.

>CASS
>(shy)
>I have met this one girl.

DOLL smiles.

>DOLL
>See, that's what you need, the love
>of a good woman! You're better
>than all this football nonsense,
>son. You could really be somebody.
>You ain't stupid, Cass.

>CASS
>(laughs)
>I hope she is though.

DOLL gives him a playful clip round the ear.

>DOLL
>(smiles)
>You just behave yourself.

DOLL hugs CASS. The moment of affection looks awkward. DOLL releases him.*

INT. CASS & FREEMAN'S FLAT, LIVING ROOM – EVENING
CASS is buttoning up his shirt while FREEMAN sits on the armchair and continuously stabs a bayonet into the table.

> FREEMAN
> What's she do then, this bird?

> CASS
> Fuck knows, travel agent or something.

> FREEMAN
> Reckon she could get us a cheap deal?

> CASS
> (laughs)
> Steady on, mate, give us a chance.
> It's my first date for fuck's sake.

FREEMAN stands up and wanders aimlessly round the room.

Performance-wise, I think this is the best scene in the film. Peter Wight especially was brilliant, because CECIL doesn't have much dialogue and the sign of a good actor is that he can still be totally convincing without it. His hand movements, his sighs and little glances were all fantastic.

The basis of the DOLL and CECIL relationship is obviously DOLL, she is the boss. We gave CECIL less dialogue to help emphasise that DOLL was the strong one. Also, there's a sense of how uncomfortable it felt at the time, because they were a lot older than CASS. There's the whole thing with CECIL going to touch CASS and not being able to. That's a recurrent theme throughout the film, there's no connection between the father and son, and that's very difficult to get across in dialogue. You'd need pages of dialogue to achieve that, but a great actor can do it in one moment. JSB

FREEMAN
I don't trust none of them, mate.
You gotta use the three F's rule
with any Reenie, Cass.

CASS looks confused. FREEMAN counts on his fingers.

FREEMAN (CONT'D)
Find 'em. Fuck 'em. Forget 'em.

CASS laughs as he puts his coat on. He feels the pockets
and starts to take out a variety of knives and knuckle-
dusters, and lays them on the table. FREEMAN starts
laughing and picks up a Stanley knife.

FREEMAN (CONT'D)
Here. You better take Uncle Stan
with yer. Just in case.

CASS contemplates then takes the knife and leaves
smiling.

INT. GREEK RESTAURANT – NIGHT
CASS and ELAINE sit at a small table reading the menu.
CASS looks nervous, thinking of something to break
the silence.

CASS
How's your mate?

ELAINE
Who, Linda? Fine. Her pride's hurt
more than anything else. She'll be
alright. I'm surprised you never
smacked that geezer after what he
said to yer, though.

CASS looks across at a MALE & FEMALE DINER at the
next table, who are staring at him. They put him on
edge as they whisper to each other. CASS looks back at
ELAINE.

CASS
Yeah, me too.

ELAINE
You the old-fashioned type then?
(impersonating a man's voice)
Nobody hits a woman when I'm
around.

CASS
(Embarrassed)
Must be.

ELAINE
I suppose I'm glad really you never
bashed the National Front cunt.
Even if he probably deserved it.

CASS smiles and shrugs.

CASS
Yeah, he probably did.

INT. ANNE OF CLEVES – NIGHT
FLASHBACK
We flash back to the welcome home party. ELAINE and
LINDA have since left. CASS, FREEMAN and PRENTICE
grab a bottle each and violently smash them over
the NF SKINHEADS' heads, and dish out a severe
beating.*

---

* A funny moment in the Greek restaurant sequence is where we flash back to the pub,
where CASS, PRENTICE and FREEMAN get their revenge on the SKINHEADS by
smashing beer bottles over their heads. I'm sure it's been noted, but the guy at the end
of the bar didn't have any reaction to the bottle being smashed on his skull! We had to
cut away from that shot really quickly. If you pause at that moment when you're
watching the DVD, you'll see the guy just sort of sits there. I don't think it was
intentional, maybe just a bit of nerves on his part. JSB

INT. GREEK RESTAURANT – NIGHT
The GREEK WAITER arrives.

> GREEK WAITER
> Have you guys decided?

> ELAINE
> I'll have the mezze please, and
> then the shish kebab. And could
> I have an ouzo please?

> GREEK WAITER
> Of course. And you, sir?

> CASS
> (rushes)
> Yeah, I'll have that as well please.

> GREEK WAITER
> Two mezze, two shish and two ouzo.

And would you like anything to go
with the shish? Any side dishes?

CASS waits for ELAINE to speak as he has no idea about
Greek food.

ELAINE.
Some taramasalata please.

GREEK WAITER
You sir?

CASS
Same please.

ELAINE realises that CASS doesn't know what he has
ordered.

ELAINE
You like mezze then?

CASS
(unconvincingly)
Yeah. You?

ELAINE
Yeah, I love the sheep's testicles best.

CASS
(concerned)
Do yer?

ELAINE
Mmmmmm, yeah. (pause) You've
never had mezze before, have you
Cass?

CASS
Nah. I've never even been out the
country, never mind eat a pair of
Greek sheep's bollocks.

ELAINE bursts out laughing.

CASS (CONT'D)
They ain't seriously going to bring
out a pair of lamb's nuts, are they?*

ELAINE continues to laugh. They're relaxed in each
other's company and she finds his naivety attractive.

ELAINE
(hesitantly)
I don't want to sound too keen or
nothing, but I got to tell you, Cass,
I can't get involved with you if
you're still going to be running
around like a bunch of kids,
fighting every weekend. My mum
and dad'd kill me.

CASS looks awkward.

CASS
(tentatively curious)
What's your old pair like then?
They alright?

---

* I remember, during preproduction, being in a Greek restaurant with the real Cass
and Elaine. Cass likes his traditional British fare, he's not the most adventurous when
it comes to food, so that bit of the character is very real! Cass went to the toilet and
Elaine ordered calamari. When Cass came back, the calamari turned up. He said,
"What's this then?" and Elaine said, "Oh, they're onion rings." He took a few calamari
rings with his steak and chips, thinking they were onion rings, and bit into them. It
was just a great example of how Elaine winds Cass up all the time. She is the boss in
the Pennant household! JSB

ELAINE gets nervous. She smiles but doesn't answer.

>   CASS (CONT'D)
>   What?

>   ELAINE
>   God knows how I'm going to
>   explain you to them.

>   CASS
>   What, 'cos of the football thing?

>   ELAINE
>   (awkward)
>   Well that as well, but . . . well, let's
>   just say they're old-fashioned.

CASS understands it's a colour issue.

>   CASS
>   What, ain't they ever met a big,
>   scary, black man before?

>   ELAINE
>   (awkwardly)
>   Not really. More ignorance than
>   anything nasty.

CASS shrugs. The MALE DINER has been continuously staring at CASS and whispers again to the FEMALE DINER. It puts CASS on edge. He looks at his watch.

>   CASS
>   (agitated)
>   Where the hell are the drinks?

> ELAINE
> (laughs)
> Calm down, give him a chance to
> pour 'em.

The MALE DINER has still not looked away and whispers again to the FEMALE DINER, who this time also stares at CASS. CASS snaps at them.

> CASS
> You having a good look, mate? You
> want a fucking photo or
> something?

The MALE DINER is taken aback.

> MALE DINER
> (cautiously)
> Sorry Cass, I was just telling the

missus about when we took the
Holte End at Aston Villa.

CASS is shocked.

> CASS
> (apologetically)
> Ah, shit. Sorry, mate. I thought you
> were looking at us 'cos of . . .

CASS points to himself and ELAINE, emphasising the
difference in colour. CASS is embarrassed and turns
back to ELAINE.

> CASS (CONT'D)
> It's difficult to tell with a lot of
> people sometimes.

ELAINE smiles at CASS and blushes.

> ELAINE
> (tenderly)
> Not me.

CASS falls for her. The GREEK WAITER arrives with the
drinks.

> FADE OUT

EXT. WEST HAM UNITED STADIUM – DAY*

PRENTICE appears and goes to walk up the street. He is returning from work and is wearing a suit. He is suddenly set upon by two men, BINGO and CP, who stab and slash him all over his face and body. The ASSASSIN is with them and looks on nervously.

INT. CASS & FREEMAN'S FLAT, LIVING ROOM – EVENING. CASS and ELAINE sit watching TV. FREEMAN enters in a hurry.

> FREEMAN
> (stressed)
> Fuckin' hell!

CASS and ELAINE look concerned.

> FREEMAN (CONT'D)
> Prentice just took a right hiding
> off some gooners.

> CASS
> Fucking gooners!? Since when did
> Arsenal have a decent fucking mob?

> FREEMAN
> I'm telling yer, Cass, he's bad, mate.

---

* This was a scene where the sound design made it a lot more violent. There's a process called ADR, which is when an actor comes into the sound studio after you've shot the film and records additional dialogue. We brought Gavin in for this scene to do some screaming reactions. Originally, we thought if it was silent it would be more chilling, but changed our minds in the edit. We also concentrated on the ASSASSIN's reactions, rather than the blood and gore of the slashing. With the focus on sound design, it appears more sinister if you can't see the injuries and you can only hear the victim being slashed. We decided to do that throughout the film during all the violent scenes, never really to dwell on the impact of the violence. We thought it was more important to tell the story and to do the dramatic sequences, spending more time on them and the character development, rather than showing a nose getting broken or a cheek getting opened up. JSB

                    CASS
                    How bad?

                    FREEMAN
                    They cut him to ribbons. Reckon
                    he needed over a thousand
                    stitches.

                    CASS
                    (grimaces)
                    Fucking 'ell. Thousand stitches?
                    What'd they do him with, a
                    chainsaw?

                    FREEMAN
                    Poor cunt looks like he's been in
                    some fucking horror film or
                    something.

FREEMAN is frustrated with ELAINE'S presence.
ELAINE notices the tension and stands up.

                    ELAINE
                    I better be going.

CASS feels awkward and is torn between them.
ELAINE walks to the door.

                    CASS
                    You alright, Elaine?

She smiles nervously then leaves.

                    FREEMAN
                    (angry)
                    What the fuck you playing at,
                    Cass?

                    CASS
                    (shocked)
                    You fucking what, mate?

                    FREEMAN
                    (frustrated)
                    Weren't it you that always said no
                    slush on the firm?

          CASS is speechless.

                    FREEMAN (CONT'D)
                    (snaps)
                    She ain't that fucking special
                    anyway, mate.

CASS goes to hit FREEMAN. They stare at each other but know what the outcome would be. CASS thumps the table instead.

>   CASS
>   Fuck sake! When we got Arsenal next?

FREEMAN calms down.

>   FREEMAN
>   Forget it, mate, the Old Bill are all
>   over it. It'll need to be away from
>   football. They'd never show at ours
>   after this anyway.

>   CASS
>   What gooner firm done him then?

>   FREEMAN
>   Some little mob out of Islington.

CASS thumps the wall.

>   CASS
>   Fucking snidey cunts!

FREEMAN walks around.

>   FREEMAN
>   They targeted him, Cass. It's all
>   getting fucking personal, mate.

CASS is deep in thought.

>   CASS
>   Let the dust settle for a while and
>   we'll pick our time carefully.

EXT. VICTORIA PARK – DAY

ELAINE and LINDA sit on a park bench and are on their lunch break from work. ELAINE is subdued. LINDA is relaxed and stares at the sky, smoking.

> ELAINE
> Did you book Mr Taylor's flight to
> Majorca, Lind'?

> LINDA
> Yeah, why?

> ELAINE
> He keeps bloody phoning up to see
> if we've done it.

> LINDA
> (laughs)
> I reckon he's a sex pest. What you
> reckon?

> ELAINE
> (distant)
> Eh? Who?

> LINDA
> (laughs)
> That slimy cunt, Mr Taylor! Waken
> up, girl.

ELAINE forces a smile.

ELAINE
Yeah.

LINDA shakes her head and stretches her arms,
yawning.

LINDA
How long's it been now then?

ELAINE
What?

LINDA leans forward and laughs.

LINDA
(mocks)
"What?" Fuck me, Elaine, you been
on the wacky baccy? You and Cass,
you stupid mare!

ELAINE
(distant)
Oh, eh? About ten months I think.

LINDA
(jokes)
Bloody 'ell, ten months? When's
the wedding? Should I buy a new
hat?

ELAINE forces a smile.

LINDA (CONT'D)
You do still like him, don't yer?

ELAINE
Yeah, 'course.

LINDA laughs.

> LINDA
> Who'd have thought you'd end up
> with some ex-con?

ELAINE doesn't react. LINDA notices something is
distracting her.

> LINDA (CONT'D)
> What's wrong?

> ELAINE
> Just this whole stupid West Ham
> thing.

> LINDA
> Oi, steady on.

> ELAINE
> No, it ain't the football itself, just
> all the violence. They're like little
> kids in the fucking playground.

LINDA
(defensive)
Well, what d'you expect him to do
when one of his closest mates gets
his face opened up? How would
you feel if it was me?

ELAINE
(anxious)
Yeah, but where's it going to end,
Lind'? He takes revenge for
Prentice and what do they do
next? It's just gonna keep going till
someone gets killed or something.

LINDA is silent but looks at ELAINE.

LINDA
(seriously)
You really love him, don't yer?

ELAINE
(frustrated)
That's the bloody problem!

LINDA still looks serious but then bursts out laughing.

LINDA
You soppy bint!

ELAINE playfully ruffles LINDA's hair as she is
embarrassed.

ELAINE
Cheeky slag!

FADE OUT

INT. MONTY'S BREAKFAST CAFE – DAY
1987

The GANG from the first scene sit having breakfast. CP sits across from BINGO, who is sitting next to the ASSASSIN. The door bursts open and CASS, FREEMAN and a heavily-scarred PRENTICE burst in with some ICF.

> PRENTICE
> (sneers)
> Good morning, gentlemen.
> Remember me?

A fight erupts. CASS heads for BINGO and continuously beats him with a metal pipe. CP stabs CASS in the groin.*

EXT. CASS & FREEMAN'S FLAT – DAY
ELAINE approaches the door and knocks. There is no answer. She takes a set of keys out, opens the door and enters.

EXT. CASS & FREEMAN'S FLAT – DAY
A Transit van speeds along into the parking area.

---

* *Monty's café – where the ICF get their revenge on the Arsenal firm – is a café in Upton Park run by a Turkish guy. Anyway, he allowed us to shoot there, but would not let us put any Arsenal memorabilia up on the walls, even though it was only for a film. He said, "This is a West Ham café, I'm sorry."*

I think it's the most violent scene in the film. We didn't have a lot of time to shoot it, so most of it was improvised. To give you an indication of how real it was: Paul Kaye broke his finger and his ribs in that fight and Gavin broke his hand. It was only the second day of filming, but that's how much effort these actors put into it. When CP stabs CASS in the groin the knife snapped in half. It was a plastic knife, so you can imagine how much effort Paul Kaye was putting into it.

I'll never forget what Cass said at the end of that day: "There is no Green Street, there is no Football Factory, and there is no ID or The Firm." The whole crew was in stitches. JSB

INT. TRANSIT VAN – DAY

CASS, FREEMAN and PRENTICE sit in the back of the van. They are high on adrenalin after the fight. CASS has been stabbed in the groin and is bleeding.

>PRENTICE
>You alright, mate? I know a doctor who's handy with the old needle and thread.

>CASS
>(winces)
>Yeah, I'll be fine.

PRENTICE bends over to look at the injury.

>CASS
>(laughs)
>It's alright, mate, you don't have to suck my cock.

They all laugh. PRENTICE thumps the side of the van in delight.

> PRENTICE
> We fucking done them gooner
> cunts!

INT. CASS & FREEMAN'S FLAT – DAY
The flat is quiet as ELAINE sits waiting for CASS. We hear voices outside the front door. ELAINE hides in the kitchen to surprise CASS. The door opens and CASS, FREEMAN and PRENTICE walk in. They are still high from the fight. FREEMAN looks at the wound and grimaces.

> FREEMAN
> You want to get yourself up the
> doctor's with that, mate.

> CASS
> (laughs)
> Nah, it's just a little scratch.

CASS winces.

> CASS (CONT'D)
> Never saw the cunt coming.
> Fucking jumped up between my
> legs. Could've cut my balls off.

The BOYS all laugh.

> ELAINE (O.S.)
> (screams)
> I wish he had cut your balls off,
> you bastard!

The BOYS stop laughing and look at each other in shock, as they realise ELAINE is in the house. CASS frowns.

CASS
(whispers)
Oh, shit!

PRENTICE and FREEMAN are still buzzing. They try to hold in their laughter like reprimanded schoolboys, but snigger. FREEMAN heads for the door followed by PRENTICE.

FREEMAN
(quietly laughs)
Sorry mate, you're on your own
with this one. I'd rather go over
Millwall on my todd than face that.

CASS
(sarcastically)
Thanks, pal.

PRENTICE has a dilemma and looks at CASS.

PRENTICE
Look, Cass, you know I'm your
mate 'n' all, but . . .

CASS shakes his head and smiles nervously.

CASS
Go on. Fuck off.

PRENTICE gives a thumbs-up as him and FREEMAN leave. CASS can hear ELAINE crying.

CASS (CONT'D)
(tentatively calling)
Elaine? Elaine, you alright?

ELAINE comes bursting through the door.

>ELAINE
>(furious)
>Alright? No, I ain't all fucking
>right, Cass. Look at the state of yer.
>You promised. You promised me
>you'd finished with all that shit.

>CASS
>(defensively)
>What?

>ELAINE
>(mocks)
>"What?" "What?" Don't you
>fucking 'what' me, alright?

She stares at him for a moment.

>ELAINE (CONT'D)
>Can't you just give it up? You're a
>grown man, Cass.

>CASS
>(defensive)
>I ain't a fucking junkie, Elaine!
>You're treating me like some kind
>of smack-head or something.

ELAINE is really frustrated and throws her arms up.

>ELAINE
>Can't you see? That's exactly what
>you are. A fucking violence addict!
>You try and hide it from the
>people who care about you most.

You tell them that you ain't, but
we all know that's what you really
are.

CASS
That's bollocks, Elaine.

ELAINE
I'm not your mum, Cass. I'm not
going to be there just to tend your
wounds after every fight. I love
you, but I don't want my kids
growing up with a dad who ain't
there.

CASS
I done my time, I ain't going back
inside, Elaine. And who the fuck
said anything about having kids?

ELAINE
I ain't talking about going to
prison. You keep going with all
this and it won't be a cell they'll
have to lock you away in, it'll be a
fucking wooden box! And anyway,
too late on the kids thing, mate.

CASS
Eh?

ELAINE
(mocks)
"Eh?"

ELAINE throws a cup at the wall in frustration.

ELAINE (CONT'D)
(shouts)
I can't believe I'm having a baby
with a fucking football thug!

The penny drops with CASS eventually.

CASS
(quietly)
Fucking 'ell.

ELAINE
Yes, "fucking 'ell"! How we going to
survive on the dole if I have to stop
working then? You got to at least
try and get some kind of job, Cass.

CASS
(defensive)
How's a black, ex-con hooligan ever
going to get a job over any of the
rest of Maggie's Millions?

ELAINE
(frustrated)
I don't fucking know. You're
supposed to be the one with all the
big ideas!

CASS goes quiet.

CASS
I could speak to Ray.

ELAINE throws her hands in the air.

ELAINE
That's all we bloody need! You
might as well reserve another
place in Wormwood Scrubs then.

CASS feels awkward. He tries to
find the right words.

CASS
I got to provide for you and this
kid though, Elaine, if we're gonna
start a family.

ELAINE is quiet for a moment.

ELAINE
Fine. You go and see Don Corleone
if you want, but I'm telling you,
Cass. You get nicked one more time
and you'll have no bloody family to
provide for.

ELAINE storms out.

INT. ALBANY NIGHTCLUB, RAY'S OFFICE – NIGHT CASS
sits across from RAY. There is a mutual respect.

RAY
You well mate?

CASS
Yeah, you?

RAY nods.

RAY
(laughs)

You still playing at toy soldiers
then, Cass?

CASS smiles.

> CASS
> (rambles)
> Yeah well, not really, mate. Trying
> to keep a low profile on that one.
> They're talking long fucking
> stretches now if you get done at
> the football. A load of Chelsea got
> done in dawn raids, so it's just a
> matter of time before they start on
> us again. The Old Bill've got these
> undercover cunts who try and mix
> in with the firm and ...

RAY interrupts.

> RAY
> What you after then, mate?

> CASS
> I got a proposition for yer.

> RAY
> I'm listening.

> CASS
> Remember you said you'd have a
> bit of work ...

RAY interrupts again.

> RAY
> Cut the bollocks out, mate. What is
> it you want?

CASS
Let me run your doors for yer.

RAY
Go on.

CASS
How many clubs you got now?

RAY
Enough.

CASS
Well, say I provide all 'enough' clubs or pubs with the best doormen in London and you only have to deal with me? Saves you fucking about with all the different firms you got. It'll cut out all the shit. One contact, one invoice, one firm.

RAY
Who you talking about? Your five hundred football squaddies?

CASS
Some of them, yeah, but not just them, Ray. All sorts of geezers.

Courses for horses kind of thing.
It's not a numbers game though,
mate. You gotta pick the right
heads for the right clubs.

RAY is silent for a while.

RAY
Let me have a think, mate. I'll let
you know.

CASS
Alright, I'll leave it with yer.

CASS leaves.*

---

* On the last night of the shoot we were in a nightclub in East Ham called Chocolate City. It's an amazing location that our location scout, Claire Tovey, found, and has this imposing gasworks behind it. The interior of it we used for RAY's office. Tamer Hassan, who plays RAY, is a confident guy, a very funny guy as well. RAY is a character based on a real person who's very well respected in the East End. Not really somebody to mess about with! We were about to start shooting this scene and Tamer was giving it the usual fun and games, so just before the first take I looked at him and said, "How are you feeling?" He said, "Oh I'm good, real good." "I'll just let you know then – RAY's wife's standing outside with the kids, looking at the monitor." The colour drained out of his face and it took the edge off him. It was hilarious. He went outside to meet RAY's wife, and he was extremely polite and respectful. 'Mrs Ray' sat next to me, beside the monitor, and was really impressed with his performance. She said that her husband, who will remain nameless and is obviously not really called 'Ray', would also be very impressed. I think he was, after he'd seen the film and met Tamer in the flesh at the premiere. JSB

INT. ANNE OF CLEVES PUB – NIGHT
CASS sits with PRENTICE and FREEMAN in a corner.

>   CASS
>   You'll have to wear a suit.

>   FREEMAN
>   (concerned)
>   A fucking suit?

CASS leans forward.

>   CASS
>   (mocks)
>   "A fucking suit?" Yes, a fucking suit!

>   FREEMAN
>   I don't have a suit.

>   CASS
>   (laughs)
>   Come on, you've got to have some
>   sort of suit?

>   FREEMAN
>   I got my court suit.

>   CASS
>   There you go. It ain't a fucking
>   fashion show, mate.

>   FREEMAN
>   (frustrated)
>   Fuck me. A fucking suit.

CASS laughs and PRENTICE takes a big gulp of his drink.

>   CASS
>   And a bowtie.

PRENTICE laughs, spitting his drink everywhere. They all crack up laughing.

> FREEMAN
> (laughs)
> You cunt!

> CASS
> (laughs)
> Just look fucking smart, alright.

FREEMAN looks at the clothes he is wearing and straightens them.

> FREEMAN
> (smiles)
> I'm always fucking smart, you
> cheeky bastard.

EXT. THE M & M WINE BAR – NIGHT
FREEMAN and PRENTICE stand at the entrance to the
wine bar in their new roles as doormen. They chat to
several PRETTY GIRLS who flirt with them.

> CASS (V.O.)
> It wasn't the same buzz as
> running with the ICF, but none of
> us could take the risk anymore.
> The courts were promising ten
> years for football hooliganism and
> the Old Bill said they had
> infiltrated every firm in London
> with undercover coppers. The boys
> moaned about it being boring, but
> it was the height of late 1980's
> greed and it helped that they were
> making loads a' money.

EXT. ALBANY NIGHTCLUB – NIGHT
CASS stands at the door with a black doorman, MR T, who looks like his namesake from *The A Team*. A group of ROWDY MALE CLUBBERS approach the door, but calm as they see the size of the doormen.

> CASS (V.O.)
> Ray wanted the biggest, blackest, baddest geezers, on his roughest doors.* It was a psychology move more than anything, but it always

---

However you imagine Frank Bruno to be is how he really is. Those who haven't read the book won't realise that Frank was a really important character in Cass Pennant's life, so we thought it would be nice to offer him a cameo part.

Frank likes to do impressions of Scottish people, which is not great if you're a Scottish director trying to tell him what to do. "Okay, Jimmy." You can imagine Bruno doing it in his voice: "Okay, Jimmy. See you, Jimmy!" He thought this was hilarious and, looking back on it, it was very funny, but at the time it was really stressing me out.

At the end of the second act, where CASS starts to work as a bouncer, you'll notice Cass Pennant and Frank Bruno playing the two doormen at the entrance to the club. He also appears at the end of the film as one of the heavies in the funeral procession. He wasn't the only ex-World Champion boxer in the film either. Charlie Magri also makes an appearance in one of the earlier pub scenes. JSB

worked and kept Ray minted and happy. More importantly, I was making clean money and keeping Elaine happy.

FADE OUT.

INT. CASS & ELAINE'S HOUSE, DINING ROOM – CHRISTMAS DAY 1992
ELAINE is heavily pregnant, and sits at the table with DOLL and CECIL. There is a big spread. Times are obviously good but DOLL now looks really unwell.

> DOLL
> Oooh, where did you get these crackers from, dear? They're lovely. Look Cecil.

DOLL shows the cracker to CECIL. ELAINE is embarrassed.

> ELAINE
> (understated)
> I only picked them up cheap.

CECIL gives an approving look.

> DOLL
> Marks and Sparks, eh? That's quality stuff, that is. I'll be all embarrassed to have you round to ours next year. We only get ours from the catalogue.

ELAINE smiles.

ELAINE
We used to always get our birthday
presents from the catalogue. Mum
would be paying it up all year, just
in time for us to order the next lot.

DOLL smiles at ELAINE and gently pats her stomach.
She obviously has great affection for her daughter-in-
law.

DOLL
Won't be long now, dear.

ELAINE
I know, two weeks.

DOLL
I said to Cecil, I think it's going to
be a girl this time, didn't I Cecil?

CECIL smiles. He's drunk.

ELAINE
D'you think so?

DOLL
'Course, you're all out at the front,
that's the biggest sign.

ELAINE
Either that or those ice cream

cravings have done too much
damage.

DOLL smiles. CASS enters. He is smartly dressed and
is carrying his son MARTIN (5 years old).

> DOLL
> Oh, would you look at them. What
> a handsome pair. Look at the
> clobber on him, Cecil.

> CECIL
> (slurred)
> Work's going well then, son?

> CASS
> Alright Dad, yeah.

> DOLL
> You keeping out of trouble though?

> CASS
> (jokes)
> I've always been a good boy, Mum,
> you know that.

DOLL and ELAINE exchange a knowing look. ELAINE tuts.
The phone rings. CASS leaves the room to answer it.

> ELAINE
> He's doing really well, Doll. You
> should be proud of him. He's a
> manager now, you know.

DOLL is impressed. She turns to CECIL.

DOLL
Manager, eh? Well if he can afford
them crackers, he must be doing
something right.

ELAINE laughs. CASS re-enters the room.

CASS
That was Ray. He's on his way over
with Martin's present.

The doorbell rings.

DOLL
(jokes)
Bloody hell, who else? You
should've bought a bigger turkey,
love!

CASS leaves the table to answer the door.

FADE OUT.

INT. CP'S BATHROOM – CHRISTMAS DAY

CP sits on the toilet holding a 'brick'-style mobile phone.

CP
(hungover)
Alright, it's me. (pause) Yeah,
happy Christmas to you 'n' all,
mate. (pause) Yeah, rough as fuck,
mate, you not go out then? Who
we got tomorrow? (pause) Nah, I'll
probably just watch it down the
boozer. (pause) Hey, you ain't going
to believe who I clocked working

on the door of this shithole club
over south London last weekend.
(pause) That black bastard that
done your brother who I stabbed
in the bollocks. Yeah.*

FADE OUT

INT. CASS & ELAINE'S HOUSE, HALLWAY – NIGHT.
1993
The front door is open and a London taxi waits outside.

> CASS
> Martin, would you record the
> football for Dad please? Your mum
> doesn't know how to use the video
> machine.

---

* I really like the way Chris Ross shot this scene with the extreme wide-angle lens. It was also great that the production design team got exactly the right kind of mobile phone, the old-style, chunky Nokia with its big aerial and huge keypad.

   We wanted CP to be doing speed and rubbing it on his gums as opposed to sniffing coke. It's another real sign of the early nineties, which complements the mobile phone. JSB

MARTIN giggles. ELAINE closes the door as the cab drives off. ELAINE turns to MARTIN as she holds her BABY DAUGHTER.

ELAINE
Right you, bedtime.*

EXT. ALBANY NIGHTCLUB CAR PARK – NIGHT
The London taxi pulls up outside the club.

INT. ASSASSIN'S CAR, ALBANY CAR PARK – NIGHT THE ASSASSIN loads the gun. His fingers are trembling and the gun shakes in his hand. CP puts his hand on the ASSASSIN's shoulder.

CP
(clinically)
Aim for the chest, not the face.

They get out of the car. We see CASS reaching the entrance, greeting BIGS and FRANK.

EXT. THE ALBANY NIGHTCLUB – NIGHT
The ASSASSIN and GANG emerge, but from the ASSASSIN'S POV.

---

* The kid that played CASS's son, Carl Fairweather, was a real find, a lovely little boy. When CASS says to him, "Tape Match of the Day, your mum doesn't know how to use the video machine," it again helps emphasise the period of the early nineties. JSB

CASS
Full house again?

BIGS
(smiles)
It was full, but he's slung half of
them out already!

CASS laughs.

FRANK
Ray's looking for yer.

CASS
(jokes)
Better be 'cos he wants to up me
fucking wages then.*

THE ASSASSIN
You black West Ham cunt.

CASS smiles and walks toward THE ASSASSIN, who pulls
out the silver gun. BANG BANG BANG! CASS is shot.

FADE OUT

FADE IN
There is pandemonium and lots of screaming. The
music has stopped and the lights are on. The picture
and sound is distorted from CASS' POV. CLUBBERS

---

* The two doormen, BIGS and FRANK, are the real Cass Pennant and a guy called Bill
Kelly, a.k.a. Mr T, who was with Cass on the actual night when he got shot. It was very
important for us to have them both there that night, guiding the actors through how
it all really happened. The shooting didn't turn out how I intended it to. We had to
improve it drastically in the sound design, to make it more threatening and realistic.
If you get to the edit and you don't have the right shots, it's amazing what sound
effects can do to enhance your scene and get you out of trouble! JSB

rush past him trying to escape as CASS attempts to scramble to safety.

FADE OUT

INT. CASS & ELAINE'S HOUSE, LIVING ROOM – MORNING
LINDA, FREEMAN and PRENTICE sit around looking after MARTIN and CASS'S BABY DAUGHTER.

> LINDA
> (crying)
> Why the fuck didn't you do something?

> FREEMAN
> We weren't even there.

> LINDA
> What's Elaine going to do, eh? If he don't make it? What about the kids?

> PRENTICE
> Just calm down, that's not doing anyone any good.

> LINDA
> (snaps)
> Don't you fucking tell me what to do.

They quieten down as they hear the front door open and close. ELAINE enters and is still in shock. LINDA's expression pleads for good news.

> LINDA (CONT'D)
> Well?

ELAINE
The Doctor says he's very lucky to
still be alive. He has three broken
ribs, a punctured lung and a
shattered collarbone. He said his
size and strength are the only
thing that's keeping him alive.

PRENTICE and FREEMAN sigh and sit, numb with relief.
LINDA hugs ELAINE really tightly and starts to cry.

ELAINE (CONT'D)
The Doctor said it's too early to say
about any permanent damage he may
have, but they'll keep a close eye on
him. He said he's a real fighter.

FREEMAN turns to PRENTICE.

FREEMAN
They must've met him before then.

FADE OUT

EXT. CASS & ELAINE'S HOUSE – DAY
A DETECTIVE and POLICEMAN stand speaking to
ELAINE. They leave and ELAINE closes the door.*

FADE OUT

INT. CASS & ELAINE'S HOUSE, BEDROOM – DAY
CASS is sleeping. ELAINE enters the room with CECIL.
They both look very emotional. CECIL smiles but is
tearful.

---

* This scene was a lot bigger in the script than it ended up being in the film. On the
day I looked at it and thought, "Oh no, this looks like something out of a soap opera."
It wasn't cinematic at all. The actors did their best to try and bring it round, but it was
just wasn't there on the page. JSB

CECIL
How you doing then?

CASS looks past CECIL to see if DOLL is behind him.

CASS
(weakly)
Alright, Dad? Where's Mum?

CECIL sits. He starts to break down.

CECIL
(crying)
How you doing?

CASS
Not bad. Where's Mum?

CECIL breaks down.

CECIL
I've got some bad news, son.

CASS realises DOLL has died.*

FADE OUT

INT. CASS & ELAINE'S HOUSE, BEDROOM – DAY
CASS sits on the bed and stares at the unopened letters.

EXT. CASS & ELAINE'S HOUSE – MORNING
A FLORIST carrying a wreath approaches the door and
rings the doorbell. CASS opens the door.

---

* It's really touching when CECIL comes to tell CASS that his mum has died, and it's a
testament to Peter Wight's acting ability again. Peter's very patient with the scenes
where he doesn't have any dialogue, and puts as much effort into them as he does into
those with dialogue. JSB

                    FLORIST
                    Delivery for Mr Pennant.

CASS takes the wreath. He is touched by someone's kindness.

                    FLORIST (CONT'D)
                    (sympathetically)
                    I'm sorry about your loss.

                    CASS
                    Thank you.

The FLORIST leaves. CASS opens the card and his face contorts. We have a close-up on the card and it reads: "Only a matter of time. Bang bang." CASS staggers with shock and falls to the ground.

INT. CHURCH, EAST LONDON CEMETERY – DAY
The small church is only half full of MOURNERS. CECIL sits alone at the front. CASS sits in the middle with FREEMAN and PRENTICE. RAY sits at the back. The VICAR finishes saying 'The Lord's Prayer'.

    VICAR
    It is at this point where I would
    like to invite any family member
    who wishes to say a few words to
    please come forward.

The silence is broken by CASS's chair squeaking, as he pushes it back to stand up. The VICAR has a puzzled look as CASS approaches the front. He is still weak after the shooting. The VICAR takes CASS to one side.

    VICAR (CONT'D)
    (awkwardly)
    I'm dreadfully sorry, but it's really
    only family members who we
    permit to speak at this point in
    the service.

CASS looks genuinely hurt.

    CASS
    But I'm her son.

The VICAR is confused and looks to CECIL, who nods his approval. The VICAR then steps back as CASS unfolds his piece of paper.

> CASS (CONT'D)
> Dear Mum. I never ever thanked
> you after all that you did for me. I
> never once told you that I loved
> you after all the love you gave me.
> I never even said goodbye, when I
> knew it was near the end. So
> thank you Mum, I love you.

CASS folds up the paper.*

EXT. CHURCH, EAST LONDON CEMETERY – DAY
CECIL shakes hands with FREEMAN and PRENTICE, who leave. CASS approaches CECIL. RAY waits in the background.

> CASS
> (subdued)
> You going for a drink then?

CECIL shakes his head.

> CECIL
> I best be off.

---

* The opening shot inside the church is almost completely symmetrical. I don't know if I've got obsessive-compulsive disorder or something, but I really love symmetrical imagery. I think that's why one of my favourite directors is Stanley Kubrick, because he used a lot of symmetry and really extreme close-ups with wide-angle lenses.

It's a beautiful scene, and it was pretty much verbatim from real life as well. It was a reminder of the identity, race and family issues that had been running throughout the film.

A friend of Cass Pennant's who played one of the mourners had sadly buried his wife a few weeks before, in that same church. She was only thirty-five years old. We only found out about it later, but it just gives an example of the spirit of the people involved in this film and what they were willing to do for us. I have so much admiration for that particular man. JSB

CECIL is crying. CASS puts his arm around him for the first time ever.*

>   CECIL (CONT'D)
>   I'm going to miss her, son.

CASS finds it hard to speak and gulps back.

>   CECIL (CONT'D)
>   You should open those letters now,
>   Cass.

CASS shakes his head. He's really emotional.

>   CASS
>   Nah, I threw them away.

CECIL sighs.

>   CECIL
>   You look after yourself, right?
>   Don't go doing nothing stupid, you
>   hear?

CASS nods. CECIL leaves. RAY approaches CASS tentatively.

>   RAY
>   You alright?

CASS shrugs.

---

* The third act is where the musical score really comes into its own, and that is what really helps to guide the film towards its conclusion.

The East London Cemetery is a beautiful location, and the performances of Nonso and Peter, showing how CASS and CECIL still couldn't connect with each other, are very subtle but extremely powerful.

There's a lot going on in that scene; visually, emotionally and musically. JSB

      RAY (CONT'D)
      We're going to get the cunt that
      shot you, mate.

      CASS
      (focused)
      When you find him, I'm the one
      that does him.

RAY pats CASS on the arm and walks off.

      RAY
      I'll be in touch.

CASS is a solitary figure in the cemetery.

INT. CASS & ELAINE'S HOUSE KITCHEN – DAY
CASS stands staring strangely at the wall. The phone
rings.

CASS
(subdued)
Hello.

No answer.

CASS (CONT'D)
Hello.

Still no answer. CASS slams the phone down. It rings again.

CASS (CONT'D)
(screams)
Hello!

No response.

CASS (CONT'D)
Fucking bastards!

He rips the phone out of the wall, throwing it at the door.

INT. WAREHOUSE – NIGHT
RAY and CASS walk round the ASSASSIN and CP, who are tied and gagged back-to-back in chairs. RAY pulls out the silver handgun and cocks it. He places it against the ASSASSIN's head and hands CASS the gun. CASS points it at the ASSASSIN. RAY speaks but his voice is the one heard previously from YOUNG PRENTICE and YOUNG FREEMAN, when YOUNG CASS was getting bullied.

> RAY
> Go on, Cass. Do him, Cass.*

---

* When RAY says to CASS in the dream sequence, "Go on Cass, do him Cass," it's a direct reference back to an earlier scene when YOUNG PRENTICE and YOUNG FREEMAN urge YOUNG CASS to punch BILLY. It's said that your childhood experiences form your adult state of mind, and that was something important that we wanted to convey through that line. JSB

The ASSASSIN screams, as does CASS, who then shoots the ASSASSIN in the head.

INT. CASS & ELAINE'S HOUSE, LIVING ROOM – DAY
CASS wakes up in a chair, stressed. The doorbell rings.

> CASS
> (shouting)
> Elaine, get the door!

ELAINE enters with the same POLICEMAN and DETECTIVE as previously. ELAINE removes the CHILDREN.

> CASS (CONT'D)
> How many times do I have to repeat it? I've got no idea who the cunt is.

The DETECTIVE is not convinced.

> DETECTIVE
> With all due respect, sir, we have
> an attempted murder suspect out
> there running around with a
> firearm. He must know half of east
> London visited you in hospital, so
> who is he going to fear most?

> CASS
> Suit yourself then, Sherlock. But
> this is all being said by you, not
> me. I told you, I don't have a
> fucking clue.

CASS shrugs. The DETECTIVE and POLICEMAN go to leave.

> DETECTIVE
> That'll be all for now then, sir.

INT. CASS & ELAINE'S HOUSE, LIVINGROOM – DAY
CASS sits with a glazed look. RAY enters with ELAINE who stands around awkwardly, realising what is coming.

> RAY
> You alright, Elaine?

> ELAINE
> (coldly)
> Yeah, you Ray?

> RAY
> Fine.

There is silence. ELAINE is trying to delay them. She knows why he is there.

ELAINE
And the kids?

RAY
They're fine.

ELAINE
Have you been ...

RAY
(interrupts)
Put the kettle on, love, would yer?

ELAINE looks at CASS, concerned. She leaves in frustration.

RAY (CONT'D)
You alright, son?

CASS stares blankly.

RAY (CONT'D)
How's the breathing?

Silence.

RAY (CONT'D)
We found him.

CASS
(strangely)
Who you found then?

RAY looks confused.

> RAY
> We found the little cunt that shot
> you, Cass. Give us the nod and it's
> done.

CASS stares into the distance. RAY takes a deep breath.

> RAY (CONT'D)
> (sincerely)
> Look, I know what you're going
> through must be hard, mate, but
> just give it a bit of thought and tip
> us the nod when you want him
> taken care of. Alright?

CASS doesn't respond. RAY stands up to leave.

> RAY (CONT'D)
> You know where we are when you
> need us. Look after yourself, son.

RAY pulls out a brown envelope and places it on the table.

> RAY (CONT'D)
> That'll keep you ticking over.

CASS does not acknowledge RAY leaving. He stares blankly.

INT. CASS & ELAINE'S HOUSE, KITCHEN – DAY
CASS stares strangely at MARTIN, who is playing with a toy car on the table. Their BABY DAUGHTER is crying in her pram. ELAINE carries plates of food to the table. CASS grabs the toy car.

          CASS
          (shouts manically)
          Stop it! Stop it!

MARTIN screams and runs into ELAINE, causing her to
drop the plates which smash on the floor.*

          ELAINE
          (shouts)
          Bloody hell, Cass! You can't just
          shout at him like that.

          CASS
          Fuck off!

---

* Most of the third act is set in CASS and ELAINE's house. It's quite difficult when
you're shooting in a real location which is really cramped, for obvious reasons. These
scenes were filmed halfway through the shooting schedule, when things start to get
stressful. It's because you don't have the euphoria of beginning a new project and you
can't see the finishing line in sight. It worked in our favour because I think it helped
the actors get into that bleak state of mind! JSB

ELAINE
What?

CASS
(roars)
Fuck off! Leave me alone!

ELAINE is frightened but tries to hold it together. Her voice breaks.

ELAINE
OK then. I'll leave you alone.

ELAINE picks up her BABY DAUGHTER and grabs MARTIN by the hand.

ELAINE (CONT'D)
I'm going to Linda's but I'm warning you, Cass. If I find that you're plotting to do that little no-mark runt that shot you, I ain't coming back.

ELAINE leaves. CASS picks up a coffee mug and smashes it against the wall. He looks wild-eyed.

INT. CASS & ELAINE'S HOUSE, BEDROOM – DAY
The house is quiet. CASS enters the bedroom. He looks

up and sees his frail reflection in the mirror. Suddenly,
THE ASSASSIN appears in the mirror holding the silver
gun. CASS is frozen with fear.*

>
> THE ASSASSIN
> (laughing)
> Hello Carol.

---

* The scene where CASS is looking in the mirror and sees the ASSASSIN appear was the
most difficult scene to shoot, because we had to do it in one shot. I'm not going to give
away the secret of how we did it, but it was all done for real, there were no special
effects. It took four hours to achieve that one shot. Chris, the DP, still says it's the most
difficult shot he's ever had to complete. JSB

The ASSASSIN's face distorts. CASS is confused and turns, but finds nobody there. CASS turns back towards the mirror and the ASSASSIN has reappeared.

> THE ASSASSIN (CONT'D)
> What's wrong, Carol? I thought you were a tough guy? You were when you nearly killed my brother. Weren't you going to do me 'n' all, Carol? Shoot me in the head, Carol? What's wrong, weren't you man enough, Carol?

THE ASSASSIN pulls out the silver handgun.

> CASS
> Come on, fucking finish me off then.

CASS turns but the ASSASSIN is not there. He turns back to the mirror and the ASSASIN has reappeared, laughing. We now hear BILLY's voice coming from the ASSASSIN'S mouth.

> THE ASSASSIN
> (Billy's voice)
> Didn't you like the flowers then, Carol?

CASS punches the mirror with full force, smashing it into pieces. He collapses on the floor crying.*

---

* We filmed a scene with Nonso where CASS has a mental breakdown. It was an amazing scene and it would have been a real potential BAFTA moment, but unfortunately it slowed the pace of the film down and we had to cut it out. It was a lesson for me that when you're writing a script you should try to be confident you're going to use pretty much everything in your final draft. I'd say we used ninety percent of the scenes we shot. The third act was where we cut most stuff out. JSB

EXT. CASS & ELAINE'S HOUSE – DAY
ELAINE and LINDA walk up the path with MARTIN and
their BABY DAUGHTER. The door is ajar. ELAINE looks
concerned and opens it slowly.

> ELAINE
> Cass? Cass?

ELAINE looks inside. There is smashed glass on the
floor.

> ELAINE (CONT'D)
> Stay here with the kids, Linda. I
> think we've been done over.

LINDA looks frightened. ELAINE enters the house.

EXT. LONDON STREET – DAY
Two black funeral cars and a hearse drive slowly down
a quiet street in procession. The windows are blacked
out.

INT. THE BLUE LION PUB – DAY
The pub is full of CUSTOMERS watching a football game
on a big screen. In the corner sits the ASSASSIN, CP and
his GANG. They act arrogantly as it's their local pub.

EXT. THE BLUE LION PUB – DAY
The funeral procession draws slowly up to the front of the pub and stops. The car door's open and we see numerous MEN from the waist down, getting out. The MEN open the back door of the hearse and remove a coffin, placing it on the ground. The coffin is opened. Inside are baseball bats, swords and axes. The weapons are chosen and hidden in their long black trenchcoats. They walk slowly to the entrance.

INT. THE BLUE LION PUB – DAY
The ASSASSIN & CP finish their pints in one gulp and slam them on the table. CP stands up to address the BARMAID and belches loudly. The GANG laugh.

> CP
> (arrogantly)
> Another round of the same please, Dave!

The GANG laugh. The BARMAID is unimpressed.*

EXT. THE BLUE LION PUB – DAY
The camera pans from the SUITED MEN's shoes up to
their faces. We reveal RAY, FREEMAN, PRENTICE, BIGS
and FRANK. They look serious and are all dressed in
black. The hearse door opens. It's CASS.

INT. THE BLUE LION PUB – DAY
The CUSTOMERS are watching the game intently when

---

* *I always wanted the sequence with the funeral hearse to look like a car commercial,
so we spent a lot of time shooting it. The production value is really high, and I think
it's the most nicely shot sequence in the film.*

    *We had a lot to get through that day and had to film the interior bar scenes also, so
I let CP and the ASSASSIN improvise their dialogue. Paul Kaye and Bronson Webb were
in free flow and were coming up with some really good stuff. Halfway through their
routine, Chris the DP walked through from the bar into the room where my monitor
was set up. I said, "What are you doing here, why are you not at your camera?" He said,
"Well, I cut." "Why the fuck did you cut?" "I thought we were going to run out of film."
It was the only time I felt, "Chris, what have you done?" and that says something for
a twenty-five-day shoot! But he was right, of course, because we had to move on and
get the rest of it completed. JSB*

suddenly they lose satellite reception. They moan their annoyance. CP throws an empty pint glass at the screen.

> CP
> (shouts)
> Fucking bollocks!

He looks at the GANG. They laugh.

The pub doors open slowly and the CUSTOMERS' expressions change to horror as CASS enters the pub followed by RAY, PRENTICE and FREEMAN. The CUSTOMERS turn their backs in fear as CASS slowly approaches the ASSASSIN and CP's GANG, who try to

escape but are cornered by RAY, PRENTICE and FREEMAN. CASS slowly places the wreath on the ASSASSIN'S head.

RAY removes a gun from his coat and hands it to CASS, who holds it to the ASSASSIN'S head then slowly points it at CP, who vomits.

CASS aims the gun back at the ASSASSIN, who starts shaking. CASS looks round the pub and sees the terror on faces of the CUSTOMERS and the GANG but also PRENTICE and FREEMAN, who are out of their league.

>   RAY
>   Come on, ain't you going to do
>   the cunt?

He stares at RAY, then shakes his head in response to the question. CASS gives his gun back to RAY, turns his back on the ASSASSIN and walks towards the door.

EXT BLUE LION PUB – DAY
CASS comes out of the pub and passes BIGS and FRANK,
who he exchanges a knowing glance with before
walking back up the street.*

** At the end of the film, when CASS walks out of the pub, if you look very closely when
he opens the door the pub's actually empty. It was a mistake. We never really thought
about it properly because we shot it first thing in the day. We didn't have the extras
on set in time, so there's nobody in there!. JSB*

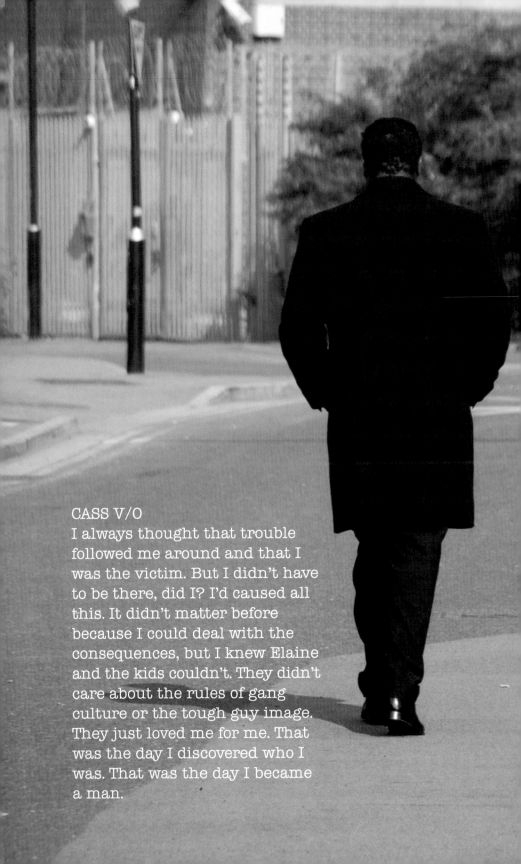

CASS V/O
I always thought that trouble followed me around and that I was the victim. But I didn't have to be there, did I? I'd caused all this. It didn't matter before because I could deal with the consequences, but I knew Elaine and the kids couldn't. They didn't care about the rules of gang culture or the tough guy image. They just loved me for me. That was the day I discovered who I was. That was the day I became a man.

FADE TO BLACK

TITLE CARDS
CASS PENNANT EVENTUALLY ACHIEVED HIS DREAM
AND HAD HIS FIRST BOOK PUBLISHED IN THE YEAR
2000.
CASS AND ELAINE REMAIN HAPPILY MARRIED.
END TITLES*

* Before the end credits start to roll, we use a photograph of Linda and Verelle, who
play DOLL and YOUNG CASS. It fades out and in its place appears a shot of the real Doll
Chambers with the real young Cass Pennant. It's a nice way to reinforce that what has
gone before is a true story. JSB

CASS: THE AFTERMATH . . .
An Interview with Jon S. Baird

You said Cass would be your first film. Did you have other scripts, other ideas?

I had a script that I'd written before Cass that I'd done with a friend of mine; a comedy based up in Scotland, which I hope is going to be my next film. We only wrote one draft so there is a lot of work still to do on it. We did about twenty-to-thirty drafts of the Cass script!

After the film was made, you were held up with a nightmare situation when your negative was spoiled.

It cost us another £80,000 to get the film repaired. Goldcrest were very supportive when the shit hit the fan. We had to go out to their postproduction facility in New York to do a lot of the repair work on the film.

What about the scenes from the film that never made the cut?

First of all, there's scene with me and the producer, Stefan, in the psychiatrist's waiting room.

Your Alfred Hitchcock cameo?

My Hitchcock cameo unfortunately never made it. There was also a really strong scene where CASS has a breakdown, just an amazing scene where ELAINE finds him rocking back and forward on the bed. There was another scene where ELAINE finds the Dr Barnardo's letters that are unopened under the bed, and confronts CASS – that never made it either. There was one hilarious scene when RAY bites a police dog. It's really funny on paper, but it just didn't work at all on film. It was a disaster! Apart from that, pretty much everything else is fully intact.

For a couple of reasons: one, creative; two, budget. Creative because we were going through a lot of time periods – the sixties, the seventies and the eighties. It was the norm to use 16mm back then for television and news footage, so we wanted to portray it as though it was really from that time period. Our DP, Chris Ross, also wanted to use it as opposed to high definition.

I would always urge a first-time filmmaker to try and shoot on film if possible. I would love to do my next one on 35mm, simply because it just looks more like a real movie. I think that when you shoot on a digital format, it doesn't matter how advanced your camera or your lenses are, the technology still isn't up to the point where it looks like actual film. It may happen in the future, but for now I'd say there is a way to go.

What about Chris Ross? Was he part of your previous gang?

Chris Ross was a new recruit for us. I'd seen *London to Brighton*, which he'd shot, and I really liked that film. Alex Buono, the DP of *Green Street*, advised me, "When you choose your DP, just make sure that when you look at him you think, 'Am I going to want to punch this guy in the fucking balls by the end of the production?'" With Chris, you kind of knew that you weren't going to do that. You knew he was just a cool character and it took a lot to rile him.

Gareth John, who was our sound recordist, was brilliant, a joy to work with. He's a very funny guy and really kept everybody's spirits up. Guy Speranza, our costume designer, is a genius! He's been assistant designer on a lot of big films; some of the Bond films, the *Batman* films and the *Harry Potter* movies.

How did you get hold of him?

Our line producer Berry Van Zwieten's wife, Jany Temime, was the costume designer for the *Harry Potter* films and she recommended Guy.

Cate Hall, the makeup designer, was relatively young, but she came along to the interview and completely blew us off our feet. Cate's an extremely intelligent young woman who knew the story inside out. She did so much research and really impressed us over other individuals who had far more experience than her.

Daniel Taylor and Dave Moyes, our production designer and film editor respectively, had both worked with me on *Casual Life*. I'd known them since way back when we were runners together, ten years previously.

They were always going to be chosen because we came through the ranks together.

Our location scout was Claire Tovey, who I'd worked with on *Green Street*. She was fantastic and found some amazing locations. Sam Leek came on as location manager after that, who I'd worked with at the BBC and on *Casual Life*. I shared a flat in the East End with Sam and Alison Marlow, our assistant producer, who I'd also worked closely with before.

Carole Salisbury, the continuity script supervisor, was like Aunty Carole to me. She was a very calming influence. Carole was really concerned about everything, that's what I really like about her.

We had the best laugh ever throughout the production. The whole crew were brilliant, a complete joy to work with.

What was the importance of them knowing the story?
It was vital that everyone in the cast and crew knew the *CASS* story. Everyone needed to have it in their soul. That's why we asked them all to read the book and to get to know Cass Pennant personally as well. If you were thinking, "It's just another job," then you weren't going to be working on *CASS*. It felt like a big family on set. I think that, whatever we all do in the future, the crew and cast of this film will keep the *CASS* movie close to their hearts. It was a special time we all shared.

What about the music in the film?
In terms of music in the film, the guy from The Beat, Dave Wakelin, was so supportive and really was a driving force behind us getting the soundtrack completed. There was so little money and everybody was saying no, because they didn't want to be associated with hooliganism. We sent Dave a personal letter explaining the film, what it was really about, how important his songs were to us. He really turned it around and got everybody else on board. We then got

Madness, The Jam, Booker T and the MGs, Harry J and the All Stars, Desmond Dekker and Ride. Ride were another band who were really supportive.

What impact do you hope this film will have?
I hope that this film becomes an important British cult movie in years to come.

I also really hope it gives encouragement to other young filmmakers. If you believe in yourself and you've got enough spirit then you can get things made, regardless of how much money you have. I hope it's also seen not just as a football hooligan film. Hopefully, people will realise that there's a lot more behind the story of *CASS* than just the ICF.

Did you think your first film would go to the West End for its opening premiere?

To have a premiere at the Empire Leicester Square, with hundreds of people turning up, was just amazing. For first-time filmmakers with a small budget it's probably unheard of, really. I was quite nervous about speaking to the press, but when it came to actually doing it I had a newfound confidence, because of the support of family and friends and everybody who'd worked on the film. It was something I'll never forget.

A Jon S. Baird Film
Written for the Screen and Directed by Jon S. Baird
Produced by Stefan Haller
Based on the book CASS by Cass Pennant and Mike Ridley

Cast

Cass . . . Nonso Anozie
Prentice . . . Gavin Brocker
Freeman . . . Leo Gregory
Elaine . . . Nathalie Press
CP . . . Paul Kaye
Assassin . . . Bronson Webb
Cecil . . . Peter Wight
Ray . . . Tamer Hassan
Martin . . . Carl Fairweather
Doll . . . Linda Bassett
Linda . . . Lorraine Stanley
Baby Daughter . . . Azaria Omaboe
Young Cass (10 years old) . . . Verelle Roberts
Freeman (14 years old) . . . Rory Jennings
Young ICF Member . . . Joe Siffleet
Bingo . . . Dave Lea
Prentice (14 years old) . . . Jayson Wheatley
Cass (14 years old) . . . Daniel Kaluuya
Stevie Hogan . . . Jamie Kenna
Shaun the Skinhead . . . Johnny Palmeiro
Marlon . . . Robbie Gee
Greek Waiter . . . Mario Demetriou
TV Presenter . . . Lucy Russell
Young Freeman (10 years old) . . . Jack Johnson
Delroy Jackson . . . Gary Lawrence
Detective . . . Helen Anderson
Sergeant Mullins . . . Ralph Ineson
Tracey . . . Gemma Baker
Vicar . . . Geoffrey Beevers
Gaffer . . . Liam Smith

Northern Comic . . . Renton Skinner

Young Prentice (10 years old) . . . Callum Ruane

Zulu . . . Winston Ellis

Teenage Bully #1 . . . Jack Bence

Pub Regular . . . Nick Bartlett

Billy the Bully . . . Brandon Robinson

Bigs . . . Cass Pennant

Frank . . . Frank Bruno

Teenage Bully #2 . . . Sid Young

Prison Guard Ron . . . Eddie Webber

Harry the Prisoner . . . Bill Gardner

Male Diner . . . Lee Turnbull

Florist . . . Tiggy Allen

Female Diner . . . Lucy Aylen

Big T . . . Bill Kelly

Prison Guard . . . Mick Robbins

Woman Passer-by . . . Sarah Finnegan

Children Passers-by . . . Eilidh Bruce, Emmy Bruce

Jock the Bulldog . . . Himself

Taxi Driver . . . Danny QPR

Joe the Barman . . . Joe Egan

Bullied Prisoner . . . Marcus Pennant

Office Worker . . . Georgina Pennant

Assassin's Gang . . . Harry Davis, Charlie French, Mark French

Greek Chef . . . Kane Manera

Crew

Co-Producer . . . Berry Van Zwieten
Executive Producer . . . Jon S. Baird
Executive Producer . . . Will Clarke
Executive Producers . . . Adam Kulick, Pierre Weisbien
Director of Photography . . . Christopher Ross
Editor . . . David Moyes
Production Designer . . . Daniel Taylor
Costume Designer . . . Guy Speranza
Hair and Makeup Designer . . . Cate Hall
Casting . . . Julie Harkin, Suzanne Smith
Original Music Composed and Performed
by Matteo Scumaci
Stunt Coordinator/Fight Choreographer . . . Dave Lea
Technical Consultant . . . Cass Pennant
Music Supervisors . . . Paul Crockford, Lisa Cope
Line Producer . . . Berry Van Zwieten
Assistant Producer . . . Alison Marlow
First Assistant Director . . . Kevin Westley
Second Assistant Director . . . Nick Simmonds
Third Assistant Director . . . Janine Frank
Script Supervisor . . . Carole Salisbury
Production Accountant . . . Jennine Baker
Production Runner . . . Harry Serjeant
Runner/Drivers . . . Eduardo Rodrigalvarez, Joe Barton-
Atkinson, Robbie Hamilton
Extras Coordinator . . . Julia Robinson
Floor Runner . . . Mango Dennis
Location Manager . . . Sam Leek
Location Assistant . . . Richard Brown
Location Scout . . . Claire Tovey
Art Director . . . Samantha Wardell
Standby Art Director . . . Amy Simons
Assistant Art Director . . . Joanna Berglund, Amy Pickwoad
Set Decorator . . . Hannah Evans
Property Master . . . Michael Povey

Dressing Props ... Ron Dowling, Michael Rawlings
Standby Props ... Stuart Read
Dialogue Coach ... Barbara Berkeley
Fight Assistant ... Felix Ntumazah
Armourer ... Chris Gudgeon
Animal Handler ... Jeff Allen, c/o Stunt Dogs
Assistant Costume Designer ... Bart Cariss
Standby Costume ... Issie Gibbons
Costume Assistants ... Natasha Cousins, James van Dyke
Hair and Makeup Artist ... Pippa Woods
Makeup Assistants ... Alex Jones, Hannah Edwards,
Nancy Sumner
Makeup Crowd Supervisor ... Liz Hart
Focus Puller ... Toby Eedy, John Watters
Clapper Loader ... Ang Richards
Camera Trainee ... Seb Lamb, Theo Berman
Steadicam Operator ... Barney Davis
Camera Truck Driver ... Robert Neill
Gaffer ... Andy Mac
Best Boy ... Paul Allen
Electrician ... Christian Hayes
Grip ... Warwick J. Drucker, David Logan
Production Sound Recordist ... Gareth John
Boom Operator ... Joe Paines
Sound Re-Recording Mixer ... Matthew Gough
Sound Re-Recording Assistant ... Antony Bayman
ADR Mixer ... Andrew Thompson
ADR Recordist ... Rob Edwards
Supervising Sound Editor ... Kevin Brazier
Sound Editors ... Ben Brazier, Robert Brazier
Action Vehicles ... TLO, Bickers Action
Stills Photographer ... Chris Burgess
EPK ... Robin Haller, Tobias Munthe
Construction ... Scene It All Services
Unit Nurse ... Millstream Nursing, Location Medical
Unit Facilities ... Wrap and Roll, Catering Set Breaks
Minibuses c/o Mark Clancy, Security Eclipse Security,

THE MOVIE

CASS

Location Assist UK
Edit Facility . . . Goldcrest Post, London
Archive . . . ITN Source
DI Finishing Services . . . Goldcrest Post Productions
DI Colourist . . . John J. Dowdell III
DI Finishing Artists . . . Peter Heady
DI Supervisor . . . Tim Spitzer
DI Producer . . . Jean Lane
Arriscan Technician . . . Cesar Mylo Hernandez
Booking Manager . . . Jeanne Sison
Video Technician . . . Ben Lay
Assistant Video Technician . . . Chris Beardsley
Digital Restoration . . . Jay Tilin
Titles . . . Worlds Away Productions, Victor Barroso
Postproduction Supervisor . . . Mike Harrop
Re-Recording Facilities . . . Goldcrest Post, London
Camera and Grip Equipment . . . Panavision, London
Lighting Equipment . . . Lee Lighting
Equipment . . . Trucks Go Trucks
Neg Development . . . Technicolor
Film Stock . . . Fuji Film UK Ltd
Lawyers . . . Lee & Thompson Solicitors
Clearances . . . Sarah Hughes
Insurance . . . Media insurance Brokers Ltd
International Sales . . . Goldcrest Independent
UK Distribution . . . Optimum Releasing

Music

'Melting Pot'
Booker T and the MG's
(Cropper/Dunn/Jackson Jr./Jones Jr.)
Courtesy of Universal Music Publishing Ltd

'The Israelites'
Desmond Dekker
(Desmond Dacres/Leslie Kong)
Courtesy of Universal Music Publishing Ltd

'The Liquidator'
Harry J and the All Stars
(Harry Johnson)
Courtesy of Universal Music. Published by
Cari-Blue Music Ltd.

'This Perfect Day'
The Saints
(Kuepper/Bailey)
Courtesy of Chrysalis Records. Published by
Ignition Music Ltd and The Saints.

'One Step Beyond'
Madness
(Cecil Bustamente Campbell, O.D.)
Courtesy of Madness. Published by Melodisc Music.

'March of the Swivel Heads'
The Beat
(Charlery/Cox/Morton/Steele/Wakelin)
© London Music (ASCAP). Administered by Warner/Chappell
Music Publishing and Warner Music UK Ltd. Licensed
Courtesy of Warner/Chappell Music Publishing (UK) Ltd
and Warner Music UK Ltd.

'Fu Manchu'
Desmond Dekker
(Desmond Dacres)
Courtesy of Universal Music. Published by
Maxwood Music Ltd.

'Land of Hope and Glory' – arrangement from
Pomp and Circumstance
Edward Elgar
Performed by Barry Wordsworth
with the BBC Concert Orchestra and the
Royal Choral Society
Courtesy of the Decca Music Group. Under licence
from Universal Music Operations. With thanks to
the Musician's Union.

'Happy Hour'
The Housemartins
(Cullimore/Heaton)
Courtesy of Universal Music. Under licence from
Universal Music Operation/Island Music Ltd.

'Down in the Tube Station at Midnight'
The Jam
(Paul Weller)
Courtesy of Universal Music. Published by Stylist Music
Ltd/Universal Music Publishing Ltd.

'Never Knew Love Like This'
Stephanie Mills
(James Mtume/Reggie Lucas)
Courtesy of Universal Music. Published by Universal Music
Publishing Ltd and Sony ATV.

'Click Click'
The Beat
(Charlery/Cox/Morton/Steele/Wakelin)
© London Music (ASCAP). Administered by Warner/Chappell
Music Publishing and Warner Music UK Ltd. Licensed
Courtesy of Warner/Chappell Music Publishing (UK) Ltd
and Warner Music UK Ltd.

'The Stripper'
David Rose
(Rose)
Courtesy of Universal Music. © David Rose Publishing Co.
(ASCAP). Administered by David Rose Publishing Co. US and
Warner/Chappell Music Publishing. Licensed courtesy of
Warner/Chappell Music Publishing (UK) Ltd and David
Rose Publishing Co. US.

'Leave Them All Behind'
Ride
(Colbert/Gardener/Queralt/Bell)
Courtesy of Ignition Records Ltd. © Creation Songs Ltd (NS)
and Damaged Pop Music (NS). All rights on behalf of
Creation Songs Ltd administered by Warner/Chappell
Music Ltd. Licensed courtesy of Warner/Chappell Music
Publishing (UK) Ltd/Universal Music Publishing MGB Ltd.

'Jackpot'
The Beat
(Charlery/Cox/Morton/Steele/Wakelin)
© London Music (ASCAP). Administered by Warner/Chappell
Music Publishing and Warner Music UK Ltd. Licensed
Courtesy of Warner/Chappell Music Publishing (UK) Ltd
and Warner Music UK Ltd.

'Theme from the S Express'
S'Express
(Gregory/Gabriel/Moore/Anthony)

Courtesy of Sony BMG. © 1989 Warner-Tamerlane Publishing Corp (BMI), May 12th Music (BMI) and Warner/Chappell Music Ltd (PRS). All rights on behalf of itself and May 12th Music administered by Warner-Tamerlane Publishing Corp. Licensed courtesy of Warner/Chappell Music Publishing (UK) Ltd.

'Step into Christmas'
Elton John
(John/Taupin)
Courtesy of Universal Music. Published by Universal/Dick James Music Ltd.

With thanks to
Skadfather Dave Wakelin
Dermalogica
Originals footwear
Episode Camden
The Daddy
Jean O'Connor
Laser Cutting Services Ltd
Pat McEnallay, Lee Lighting
Newham Film Office
Chocolate Entertainment UK Ltd
The Britannia Pub
Jim Carn
Frank McAvennie
Paul 'Bubbles' Colborne
Ian 'Butch' Stuttard
Ranald Graham
Charlie Magri
Little Jela
Bob Morris
Jeff 'Stinky Turner' Geggus
Micky Geggus
Barry 'Chicken Run' Haynes
Yvette Rowland

Ed the Shed
Laxley Pennant
Stilks
Mark Chester and Naughty Forty
Gilroy Shaw and Mad Dog Wolves
Fez and Boro Frontline
Keith 'Cuddles' Batchelor
Mark Wilson
Brett Tidman
E16 Danny Brown
Black Danny Brown
Barry Pinkus
David Richards
Keith Price
Danny Kelly
Sandy MacKendrick
Supporters of West Ham United

With special thanks to
Astrid Baird
Elsa Baird
Jane Bruce
The Haller Family
Gary Bruce
Felix Ntumazah and Black Wally
The Bowers family and friends at the Peacock gym
Elaine Pennant
Monty's café staff
T Cribb & Sons
Mick Joyce and the Hollywood East regulars
The Rob Roy Reds
To all our friends who helped make this happen

Dedicated to
John G. Baird (1934 - 2005)